NEW SWAN SHAKESPEARE

GENERAL EDITOR
BERNARD LOTT M.A.

★

Macbeth

NEW SWAN SHAKESPEARE

Macbeth

Julius Caesar

Twelfth Night

Richard II

A Midsummer Night's Dream

The Merchant of Venice

Henry V

As You Like It

Romeo and Juliet

Henry IV Part I

WILLIAM SHAKESPEARE

Macbeth

EDITED BY
BERNARD LOTT, M.A.

LONGMAN

LONGMAN GROUP LIMITED,
Longman House, Burnt Mill, Harlow,
Essex CM20 2JE, England
and Associated companies throughout the world.

First published 1958
New impression 1959
Second edition (with introduction and additional notes)
1960
New impressions 1961; 1962; 1964;
*Third edition (with illustrations in text) *1965*
*New impressions *1965; *1966 (twice);*
**1967 (twice); *1968; *1969; *1970 (twice);*
**1972; *1974 (twice); *1975; *1976 (twice); *1977;*
†1978 (twice); †1979 (twice); †1980; †1981; †1982; †1983;
This impression 1984

ISBN 0 582 52711 2

Illustrations by H.C.McBeath
Cover illustration by Caroline Holmes-Smith

We are indebted to the University of London for per-mission to reproduce extracts from the English Literature papers of the General Certificate of Education, Ordinary Level.

Printed in Singapore by
Selector Printing Co Pte Ltd

INTRODUCTION

The purpose of this book is to give and explain, in the simplest way, the text of one of Shakespeare's plays. The text itself is complete; notes and a glossary have been added to help the reader to understand the play. To get the greatest pleasure from it, he will need to learn something about the background of the play and the age in which it was written—and perhaps about Shakespeare himself, for example, or about drama as an art—but his first duty is to understand what the characters are saying and doing, and why they say and do these things.

With this end in view, and to ensure that the help given will in fact simplify the difficulties which are now met with in reading Shakespeare, explanations have been given within the range of a specially chosen list of 3,000 most commonly used English root-words. Every word in the book which falls outside this list is explained. This is done in the following way:

Words which are not used in everyday Modern English as Shakespeare used them, or which are not now used at all, will be found explained in notes on the pages facing the text;

Words which are still used in ordinary modern English with their meanings unchanged, but which are not among the 3,000 root-words of the chosen list, will be found explained in the glossary at the back of the book.

References to one or other of these places, and a study of section 2 of this introduction, should be sufficient to remove all difficulty in the understanding of the text. Explanations of longer passages are also given within the range of the word-list.

The rest of this introduction is arranged under the following headings:

v

Two Scottish generals, Macbeth and Banquo, while riding home after a victorious battle against an army of rebels, are met by three witches. These foretell that Macbeth shall be king of Scotland and Banquo the father of many kings. Macbeth is strongly influenced by their words, and his wife gives him so much encouragement that he is persuaded to murder Duncan, the king of Scotland, while he is a guest at their castle. Macbeth is now the most powerful man in the kingdom, and takes the throne. But he feels his position unsure, and suspects those around him; this drives him to the murder of Banquo, whose ghost haunts him. For the second time, Macbeth sees the witches, who warn him against the nobleman Macduff, but nevertheless persuade him to go on by telling him that "none of woman born" can harm him, and that no one will defeat him "till Birnam forest come to Dunsinane". Macduff has meanwhile gone to England to help in collecting an army to fight Macbeth, and in his absence his family is murdered by order of Macbeth.

Lady Macbeth, much disturbed in her mind, walks in her sleep, and speaks again her part in the crimes she has committed. She dies while a force, led on by Duncan's son Malcolm, and with English support, is besieging Macbeth's castle. The king realises that his position is desperate, but never loses courage, even when he finds that the witches' words have deceived him (for the forest *does* seem to move). And he is killed in hand-to-hand fighting by Macduff (who says that he was not "born of woman"). Malcolm then becomes king of Scotland.

2 *The Language and Imagery of the Play*

The English of Shakespeare's time was in many ways different from the English we speak today. A number of words or parts of words are listed below which are seldom used today as Shakespeare used them, but which occur so often in the play that it would waste space to explain them every time they appear. These words have either changed in meaning since Shakespeare's day, or fallen out of use altogether in everyday Modern English, or are shortened forms which Shakespeare used for some special effect, e.g. so as to fit in with the metrical pattern of the lines.

(No attempt should be made to learn this list by heart; it is to be consulted when difficulties occur which are not explained in the notes.)

anon – "at once".
ay – "yes".

cousin, coz – any close relative (not necessarily the child of an uncle or aunt).
e'er – "ever".
ere – "before".
'gainst – "against".
'gins – "begins".
hence – "from this place".
hither – "to this place".
methinks – "it seems to me".
mine – (sometimes) "my".
morrow – "tomorrow".
ne'er – "never".
owe – (sometimes) "own".
presently – "at once".
pr'ythee – "please" (short for "I pray thee").
quoth – "said".
sooth – "truth".
still – (sometimes) "always".
't – "it"; e.g. *under 't* – "under it".
th' – "the".
thee – "you" (singular).

thence – "from that place".
thereafter – "after that".
thither – "to that place".
thou – "you" (singular).
This is the word often used as the second person singular subject; the verb associated with it ends in *-est* or *-st*, e.g.
"And that which rather *thou dost* fear to do . . ." (I.v.22).
The verb *to be* and a few others are, however, irregular in this respect, e.g.
"*Thou 'rt* (i.e. Thou art) mad to say it" (I.v.29)
"*Thou shalt* get kings" (I.iii.67).
we, us, our – "I, me, my"; kings often refer to themselves in this way.★
whence – "from which place".
wherefore – "for which reason" (compare *therefore* – "for this reason").
whiles – "whilst".
whither – "to which place".
ye – "you" (plural).

"of" is sometimes shortened to *o'*, and "is", "was" to *'s*.

★ Malcolm begins to use these plural pronouns even before he is made king (e.g. at V.vi.4).

Like all poets, Shakespeare employed language in a way which is not usual for the making of direct statements in prose. A great deal of what he wrote is in fact not prose but verse. The lines of verse which he put into the mouths of his characters generally follow a fixed pattern of stressed and unstressed syllables; e.g.

      /   /   /   /   /
Methought I heard a voice cry, "Sleep no more!

     /   /   /   /   /
Macbeth does murder sleep," – the innocent sleep . . .
                                   (II.ii.34–5),

in which the rhythm depends upon five stressed syllables in each line. This may be taken as the normal arrangement, but completely regular rhythm, which would be dull and monotonous to listen to, is avoided by varying the positions of the stressed syllables in the lines, as in

          / /   /   /   /
Which the eye fears, when it is done, to see (I.iv.53);

or a rhythmic stress may fall lightly on an unaccented syllable, as in

     /   /   /   /   /
But screw your courage to the sticking-place (I.vii.60).

Occasionally lines rhyme in a couplet, i.e. two lines next to one another; this is particularly common at the end of a scene or of a long speech. The first scene of Act II, for example, ends with the couplet:

Hear it not, Duncan; for it is a *knell*
That summons thee to heaven or to *hell* (II.i.63–4).

Macbeth is one of Shakespeare's later plays, and shows great freedom in the arrangement of the lines; his earlier plays, on the contrary, are much more regular metrically. The three parts of *Henry VI*, for example, have only a few lines which vary the rhythm of the five stressed syllables.

The poetic use of language is also characterised by imagery, which adds to ordinary statements visions of something different, but at the same time similar in some respects. Imagery may be expressed by the use of *simile* or *metaphor*.

A *simile* is a direct comparison between the subject itself and the image which that subject recalls; e.g. Macbeth, at the end of the play, meets his enemies on the field of battle, and fights them hand-to-hand, and, speaking of himself, says:

> I cannot fly,
> But, bear-like, I must fight the course (v.vii.1–2).

Here he compares himself with a bear being baited to death. He, like a bear tied to a stake, must fight to the end, for he cannot escape.

A *metaphor* suggests a comparison without directly making it. Words used metaphorically refer at once to two or more different things, usually recalled together by the speaker in a moment of strong feeling. *Macbeth* has a great number of metaphors, and these are particularly common in the longer speeches. For example, Banquo, thinking of what the witches had told him about himself, says:

> . . . myself should be the root and father
> Of many kings   (III.i.5–6).

He thinks of the prophecy made about him by the witches; what the third witch in fact said was:

> Thou shalt get kings, though thou be none (I.iii.67),

but he changes the message into a metaphorical statement by thinking of himself as a root, which is not a tree but from which the tree grows, with its branches spreading out and carrying seed which will itself produce more trees in time. In the same way Banquo will have children and grandchildren and so on, and among them will, the witch says, be many kings. He does not say he is like a root, or that he looks like one; he simply says that he is to be "the root . . . Of many kings".

The effect of an image is often heightened by an awareness that certain ideas run through the whole imagery of the play, binding it organically as the plot does. In *Macbeth* a great deal of the imagery refers to clothing and the covering up of the body with cloth of some kind. When Macbeth begins to lose his power, and people know for certain that his rise to kingship was made possible only by murder, Angus says of him:

> now does he feel his title
> Hang loose about him, like a giant's robe
> Upon a dwarfish thief (v.ii.20–2).

When Macduff says:

> (Macbeth) is already named (King), and gone to Scone
> To be invested (ii.iv.31–2)

he is using a metaphor which is part of the common language, for *to invest* means "to give a title as an honour" with the idea that with the title go the clothes which are appropriate to it. In the same way, when Rosse tells Macbeth he has been made Thane of Cawdor, Macbeth asks

> why do you dress me
> In borrowed robes? (i.iii.108–9).

And a few lines further on Macduff continues the metaphor by referring to the old times, before Macbeth became king, as "our old robes" (ii.iv.38; see note 35 on p. 88).

There are many other instances, often more subtle than these. Angus wonders whether the Thane of Cawdor whom Macbeth fought in the battle

> did line the rebel
> With hidden help and vantage (i.iii.112–13),

which suggests the lining or strengthening sewn in under the cloth when clothing is made. And when Lady Macbeth is planning the murder of Duncan, she asks "thick night" to *pall* or wrap itself in the smoke of hell; and a moment afterwards she speaks of "the *blanket* of the dark" (i.v.48–9, 51). A good deal of this imagery is described in the notes, and more is to be found in the play; its subject-matter helps to bind the play together artistically, and adds greatly to its interest and beauty. A poet naturally deals in images, since it is his business to make his hearers (or readers) see things with fresh eyes. A new, unexpected comparison or series of comparisons is one of the best ways to this end, and Shakespeare is a master of imagery.

Most of *Macbeth* is poetry, and the kind of striking and beautiful imagery illustrated above is a particular property of great poetry. The only prose passages of any length in the play are the speeches of the Porter in II.iii. This indicates Shakespeare's general practice: prose is used for the humbler and comic characters, while the nobler ones use verse. Since *Macbeth* is concerned almost entirely with men and women of noble birth, nearly all the play is in verse. Lady Macbeth, in v.i, speaks prose when she recalls in her sleep-walking the actions she has taken part in; and Lady Macduff uses prose when she talks to her son (IV.ii), even though the emotion of this scene is intense. An exception to this rule is the scene in which Banquo is murdered; here the Murderers have some beautiful lines of poetry to speak:

> The west yet glimmers with some streaks of day:
> Now spurs the lated traveller apace,
> To gain the timely inn . . . (III.iii.5–7).

Although Shakespeare wrote for the theatre, not for silent readers, and we must, when we are reading his plays, always try to visualize them as they appear on the stage, he was also, in the best sense, a dealer in words, and to watch his language at work is the best way to understand him well. The play itself shows how great was his interest in words, for Macbeth's confidence rests in two forms of words, one about men born of woman and the other about Birnam wood moving. He finds at last that the words without the spirit behind them have deceived him, and, when he realizes that he is trapped and doomed to die, he curses the supernatural powers which have led him astray:

> be these juggling fiends no more believed,
> That palter with us in a double sense,
> That keep the word of promise to our ear,
> And break it to our hope (v.viii.19–22).

3 The Play as Drama

As we read a play of Shakespeare, we may sometimes forget that what we have before us is not essentially a book at all, but the words of a play, something which was written to be spoken and acted on the stage of a theatre. A reading of the play cannot be fully successful unless this is kept in mind, and the student should therefore take every opportunity of speaking the lines aloud rather than reading them silently. We cannot all be actors, nor have all of us the time or ability to learn long speeches. But we can, perhaps, read parts together or "stage" some striking scenes, even if it means acting with book in hand, and in doing this try to imagine the play as it might appear on the stage.

One cannot go very far in this living presentation of the play without realising that the theatre for which it was written differed in some ways from our own. For example, the stage in Shakespeare's day stretched far out into the open space where the audience sat or stood – so far, in fact, that they were gathered round three sides of it. The fourth side extended back a considerable way, and formed a recess which was roofed over by a second floor. A good deal of action could be set on the upper floor itself; in the murder scene (II.ii) Macbeth might go up to Duncan there, and whisper to his wife below when the murder is done; and here Lady Macbeth might walk in her sleep (V.i).

This old type of stage was most suitable, too, on the occasions when an actor speaks to himself, so as to let the audience know what he is thinking, or speaks directly to the audience. Such passages often occur in Shakespeare's plays; and in his time the actor who was to speak them could walk to the front of the stage, in close contact with the audience, but at a distance from the other actors. It was, therefore, unnecessary for him to speak in other than his ordinary voice. When Macbeth was left alone after the murder of Duncan (II.ii), he could express his thoughts and his horror in such a way that those watching him seemed to be overhearing the words of a man who had come amongst them. His vision of the dagger (II.i) could likewise be acted in close touch with the audience.

As far as is known, no stage lighting and practically no scenery were used in Shakespeare's theatre, and this, as it happens, was to our advantage. For in place of painted scenery, Shakespeare put into the mouths of his characters splendid descriptions, poetry which paints the scenes in the mind's eye. Banquo tells us enough about the setting of Macbeth's castle (I.vi) to bring its spirit of calm before our eyes. Nightfall is described by Macbeth (III.ii) so vividly that the actual dimming of lights would be unnecessary.

It is natural to wonder where Shakespeare found the material for the story of Macbeth, and to wonder also whether any of it actually happened in history.

A Macbeth did, in fact, live in Scotland about the middle of the eleventh century; he, with Macduff, Duncan, Malcolm and Macdonwald, appear in a number of old works on the history of Scotland. But each of these sources tells a somewhat different story, and it is certain that Shakespeare's main source was one particular book, Raphael Holinshed's *Chronicles of England, Scotland, and Ireland*; Shakespeare used the second edition of this book, which was published in 1586. He did not feel in the least bound to follow Holinshed's story, however, and the details of one incident in the play are often taken from another incident in the book; for example, Donwald murders King Duff in the *Chronicles*, and the circumstances of this murder are taken over by Shakespeare to support his story of the murder of Duncan. There is, of course, nothing wrong in this, because Shakespeare is making a play, not writing history, and the interest of the plot lies in the way the incidents are brought together to make a complete and quickly-moving story.

Although the play *Macbeth* was not published until 1623, in the great collection of Shakespeare's plays known as the First Folio, there is evidence within the play and also in other places that it was written some years earlier, in or about 1606. In that year references to *Macbeth* begin to be made in other (dated) plays, and certain passages in the play undoubtedly refer to James I as the reigning king, or were written to please him. Examples of such references are explained in note 73 on page 152, and note 111 on page 180.

4 *The Construction of the Play*

Macbeth is perhaps the easiest to follow of all Shakespeare's plays. It is constructed in such a way that almost everything which takes place refers directly to the main story, that of Macbeth's rise to power and his downfall. In the first half of the play Macbeth is shown as a noble soldier who, encouraged by natural events (his rise to power as a soldier) and supernatural ones (his meeting with the "weird women" on the heath) kills the king so that he may become king himself. When he fears failure his wife is at his side to urge him on, and together they carry out the murder of King Duncan while he is staying at their castle. Macbeth becomes king, but feels unsafe until Banquo, a truly noble and gracious soldier, is dead and can no longer influence the minds of the people against their new ruler.

The climax of the play occurs in Act III, Scene iii, where Banquo is killed by murderers whom Macbeth has hired, and Fleance, Banquo's son, escapes. This means that Macbeth is safe for the moment; he is king, as the witches prophesied. But Banquo's son is alive, and can therefore continue his line, which, as the witches showed, was to bear many kings.

After this climax, the forces ranged against Macbeth quickly become more powerful. In England, King Duncan's son is promised aid in his fight against Macbeth; in Scotland, the people are appalled at the cruel murder of Macduff's wife and children after Macduff himself has joined the forces against Macbeth. Within Macbeth's castle his wife is deranged in mind because of the deeds she has taken part in, while Macbeth himself seems to grow braver as the opposition becomes stronger. Outside the castle the people join forces against their king, and, in the final short scenes, Macbeth fights them until he meets Macduff face to face. Macbeth is killed and Malcolm, the rightful heir of Duncan, is declared king in his place.

There is nothing in the play which can be looked upon as a secondary plot. The scenes in which the witches appear encourage Macbeth and, as he learns at the end, deceive him. The scene in England shows how the forces opposing Macbeth are being built up. The murder of Lady Macduff and her children is a display of Macbeth's ruthless cruelty. Perhaps only the testing of Macduff (IV.iii) and the account of the king's miraculous power over the "king's evil" lie a little to one side of the main stream of the story. The first of these incidents is taken from Holinshed, and would have seemed more important to Shakespeare's audience than it does to us, since fear of usurped power and deceit among rulers played a great part in their minds; and the second matter was certainly agreeable to King James I, who was interested in the supernatural and would like a reference to the supposed divine power placed in a king. But in general the play moves fast and direct; it tells of a hero moving to his destruction, and its ultimate power depends on its unswerving movement. As Macbeth dominates the drama, so the plot is essentially the progress of his kingship.

It is generally agreed that some parts of the play as we now know it were not written by Shakespeare, but were added to the original by another hand. The most important of these additions is Act III, Scene v, which, as suggested on p. 134, presents a view of Macbeth agreeing neither with what comes before nor with what follows. Most editors believe that Hecate's lines at IV.i.39–43 are likewise by another writer. Each of these passages includes the mention of a song by its title only. These songs appear in full in a play called The Witch, written, at about the same time as Macbeth, by Thomas Middleton, and some have thought that it was Middleton who wrote the additions to Macbeth. Perhaps Macbeth and The Witch were being presented by the same actors at about the same time, and, when the plays were taken down in writing, there was some confusion between the two.

The construction of the whole play may have been affected by these additions. A theatrical entertainment must not be too long for the audience to watch and enjoy at one time, but it must not be so short as to send them away disappointed. It has therefore been suggested that some parts of the original play were removed when the extra scene and lines were given to the witches. If this is true it may help to explain some points in the play which appear inconsistent. In the original play there might, for example, have been a longer account of the battles against the rebels, in which Macbeth so distinguished himself, and this might have explained why Macbeth met and defeated the king of Norway and the traitor Cawdor in the battle (I.ii.53–60) and yet later he tells the witches that the Thane of Cawdor "lives, A prosperous gentleman" (I.iii.72–3). It is very likely that Cawdor was fighting for the invaders in secret, as Angus suggests a short while after:

> Whether he was combined
> With those of Norway, or did line the rebel
> With hidden ("secret") help and vantage . . .
> I know not (1.iii.111–14)

—but we cannot be certain. Again, we are not told fully of the plotting of Duncan's murder. Many lines suggest that Lady Macbeth believed she would herself kill the king; she says,

> Come, thick night, . . .
> That my keen knife see not the wound it makes . . .

and, to her husband when he arrives,

> . . . you shall put
> This night's great business into my despatch;

and

> Leave all the rest to me (1.v.48, 50; 65–6; 71).

All this might possibly mean that she would manage everything, and Macbeth would actually kill Duncan; but Macbeth must, at some time before this, have discussed the plan with his wife, since she asks him later

> What beast was 't then
> That made you break this enterprise to me?
>   (1.vii.47–8).

It seems not impossible that something is missing here, but that need not harm our enjoyment of the play. In the incident with Cawdor, the dramatic point is the fulfilment of the witches' prophecy; in the plotting of Duncan's murder, we are shown the complete understanding which exists between Macbeth and his wife.

5 The Characters

Macbeth himself dominates the drama; the play is his, for it is the story of his rise and fall. Before he first appears he is spoken of as brave and noble, and Duncan willingly honours him as a trusted lord; he calls him "valiant cousin" and "worthy gentle-man". But his character, like the day he speaks of when we first see him, is "foul and fair", and his figure is truly tragic, for he is a man, not wholly bad, against whom the forces of evil are too strong, and their temptations too attractive.

He is ambitious, and the witches he suddenly comes upon when he first appears in the play are an image of the evil forces which encourage this ambition. He lusts for power and they prophesy he will be king. To Macbeth these prophecies can be neither good nor bad; for if bad, how could they so soon begin to come true? And if good, why do his thoughts so soon turn to the idea of murdering King Duncan and taking his place on the throne of Scotland? Throughout the play Macbeth continues to give serious thought to the moral aspects of his actions, and he is in no sense an unfeeling villain without conscience or sense of nobility. This is shown when he wants to talk over with Banquo the prophecy of the witches:

> Think upon what hath chanced; and at more time,
> The interim having weighed it, let us speak
> Our free hearts each to other (I.iii.153–5).

It is felt in many other places, leading him to an expression of the condition of damnation: thinking of the consequences of his crimes, he says he will not worry about what might happen to him in the next world so long as he is granted peace of mind in this:

> that but this blow
> Might be the be-all and the end-all here, . . .
> We'd jump the life to come (I.vii.4–5, 7).

But even this is impossible, and he knows it. He makes up his mind to go no further with plans for the murder of Duncan. His wife, however, persuades him to go forward—Holinshed writes of her as "burning in unquenchable desire to bear the name of a queen"—and after some agreement between them, Macbeth kills his king while he is a guest in Macbeth's castle. By this crime Macbeth has bought the kingship through evil, and sold his soul to his ambition. Although many must doubt his honesty, no one is brave enough to defy him openly when he kills the grooms to make it seem that they are guilty. Even the lines which Macbeth speaks when he announces the murder ring false and hollow, and arouse the suspicions of Malcolm and Donalbain, who flee from Scotland. Macbeth is quick to notice this, and turns suspicion on to them:

> our bloody cousins are bestowed
> In England and in Ireland; not confessing
> Their cruel parricide (III.i.29–31),

but his real fears now lie in Banquo, whose "royalty of nature", bravery and wisdom recommend him as more suited to kingship than Macbeth. Again Macbeth makes plans to have suspicion placed on his victim; he persuades the two murderers that they are being downtrodden by Banquo.

The climax of the play is the scene in which Banquo is murdered according to Macbeth's instruction. Macbeth himself has had many uneasy feelings about the crime, but in the end it is he who, in effect, tells his wife not to worry:

> Be innocent of the knowledge, dearest chuck,
> Till thou applaud the deed (III.ii.46–7).

He should then feel safe from all his enemies, but fate quickly descends upon him in a most horrible form. At the banquet prepared as if to celebrate Macbeth's feeling of final safety, Banquo's ghost comes to haunt him. This is a terrible punishment both for his crime and also for the evil pretence of expecting Banquo to be at the banquet. Lady Macbeth cannot see the ghost, but, such is the sympathy between her and her husband, she knows or guesses all that has happened, and begins to make excuses for him. He cannot support her in her own pretence, and when the ghost appears a second time Macbeth loses his nerve.

He now stands in great need of encouragement and goes to the witches to get it. They show him apparitions which give him promises concerning his fate, but the last apparition is none other than Banquo's ghost, which brings Macbeth back to his latest crime. The prophetic promises turn out to be as evil as the murders; Macbeth is "possessed", and, knowing he is now too far gone in crime to turn back, he vows that in future he will think and act at the same time:

> From this moment
> The very firstlings of my heart shall be
> The firstlings of my hand (IV.i.146–8).

After this, Macbeth's touches of humanity become rarer. The murder of Lady Macduff and her children is possibly even more horrible than his other crimes, because it seems carried out simply to accord with his vow, and without the least reason. He is driven into his castle of Dunsinane and eventually fights with the ferocity of a wounded animal. When he is told of his wife's death his humanity momentarily returns. He thinks of the passage of life, so rapid and apparently so meaningless, and is awoken to the immediate situation by the message that the wood of Birnam is in fact moving. The first evil promise of the witches has proved worthless; but he fights on, only to meet at last his enemy Macduff, whose family he has so needlessly killed. Macduff kills him, and the second of the witches' promises is shown also to be worthless. To the end Macbeth fights bravely and this bravery is something outside the sense of safety which the witches' promises had given him. But evil has killed hope in him, and he meets his death because he has put his trust in what was either evil or worthless. Banquo's warning had once shown him the danger, but he had been either unwilling or unable to respect it:

> The instruments of darkness . . .
> Win us with honest trifles, to betray 's
> In deepest consequence (I.iii.124–6).

Duncan is, with Banquo, in striking contrast to Macbeth. As king of Scotland, Duncan is taken to be an old man, and appears in the play to be honourable, trusting and humble in carrying out the duties of his position. We see him first when his country is hard-pressed by invaders from Norway and rebels at home. In this struggle Macbeth distinguishes himself as a great fighter, and Duncan hears good reports of him with great pleasure. But what the king says of the rebel Thane of Cawdor shows his own particular difficulty: he is too trusting, too ready to accept what seems to be true:

> There 's no art
> To find the mind's construction in the face:
> He (Cawdor) was a gentleman on whom I built
> An absolute trust (I.iv.11–14).

Duncan is, therefore, powerless when he has to face evil, and he puts himself gently and meekly into the hands of Macbeth and Lady Macbeth, his host and hostess, without taking the normal precautions of having an armed guard posted near where he is sleeping. The two attendants he has by him have, like him, enjoyed a good party, and are sleepy and useless. The king goes to rest, well fed and happy in his hostess's assertions of loyalty and friendship towards him. He is murdered in his sleep by Macbeth. Duncan has proved to be fatally easy ground for his followers to plant their ambitions in. It is Lady Macbeth who has in the end some sort of finer feelings about him:

> Had he not resembled
> My father as he slept, I had done 't (II.ii.12–13).

Banquo, like Duncan, is pictured as good, brave and gracious. Both these men are, because of their positions and their honourable natures, great dangers to Macbeth in his ambitions, for their goodness contrasts too plainly with his wickedness. Like Duncan too, Banquo trusts too readily in appearances; they are both too easily deceived into thinking all is well in Macbeth's castle because its situation is attractive:

> This guest of summer,
> The temple-haunting martlet, does approve,
> By his loved mansionry, that the heaven's breath
> Smells wooingly here (I.vi.3–6).

Banquo is close to the king and also to Macbeth; he arrives with Duncan at Macbeth's castle, and, when the party for the king is over, he meets Macbeth after midnight and shows that his thoughts are full of the prophecy of the witches, whom he and Macbeth came upon at the beginning of the play. They have no time to talk at length, yet Banquo has already sensed something evil springing up in Macbeth's mind, for he says, half to himself, half to Fleance:

> merciful powers!
> Restrain in me the cursèd thoughts that nature
> Gives way to in repose! (II.i.7–9).

When Macduff discovers that Duncan has been murdered, Banquo, unlike Macbeth, expresses his grief simply and from the heart. He soon voices his suspicions of Macbeth:

> Thou hast it now, King, Cawdor, Glamis, all,
> As the weird women promised; and, I fear,
> Thou playedst most foully for 't (III.i.1–3).

But he does nothing; perhaps he is satisfied for the moment to watch events, and in any case he too is concerned in the witches' prophecies. But for this he is given no time. Macbeth quickly convinces two murderers that Banquo is the person who in secret makes them suffer cruelty and injustice, and, when Banquo is returning with his son in the evening after a day away from the castle, he is murdered. Macbeth pretends that he is expected at the banquet arranged for that evening, and his ghost, covered in blood, comes and sits in Macbeth's own chair. Macbeth is overcome with the horror of the apparition, and the party breaks up.

He is, nevertheless, to see Banquo once again. The witches show Macbeth eight kings, with many more reflected in a mirror, and the ghost of Banquo following them. This signifies to Macbeth that, although Banquo has been murdered by his orders, Fleance, Banquo's son, has escaped, and is destined to be the father of a line of kings; although Macbeth has won the throne, it is foretold that his children will never follow him in a royal line.

Macduff is the nobleman who discovered the murder of Duncan. Commanded to call early on his king, he enters the king's chamber and quickly returns with horror in his eyes and voice. Macbeth pretends not to understand him. It is Macduff who first expresses surprise at Macbeth admitting that he had himself murdered the grooms who were attending the king. "Wherefore did you so?" he asks, and since he does not seem to be convinced by Macbeth's answer, Lady Macbeth pretends to faint so that attention is drawn away from her husband. Macduff asks help for her. But his suspicions are aroused; he leaves for his own part of the country and then makes his way to England.

His wife and children are left behind in Scotland, and Lady Macduff is unable to understand his flight. Rosse tries to persuade her that her husband has left for the good of the country, and implies that he is in England to raise forces to oppose the tyrant Macbeth. Rosse says he is

> noble, wise, judicious, and best knows
> The fits o' th' season (IV.ii.16–17).

But this is no comfort to his wife, who is killed with her children by order of Macbeth.

In England Macduff has met Duncan's son, Malcolm, and at first Malcolm wishes to test Macduff's loyalty; he is afraid that Macbeth may have sent Macduff to trick him into telling his secret plans for an attack. Macduff, an honest and straight-forward person, is at first quite confused at Malcolm's words, since Malcolm makes himself out to be even more evil than Macbeth. But when all is explained, Rosse enters and announces a more bitter tragedy, the murder of Macduff's family. He cannot believe that so purposeless a crime is possible:

> All my pretty ones?
> Did you say all?—O hell-kite!—All?
> What, all my pretty chickens, and their dam,
> At one fell swoop? (IV.iii.216–19).

At first he had been unable to express his sorrow in words; now he tells his determination to take revenge on Macbeth, and to do it quickly.

The First Apparition called up by the witches had warned Macbeth of Macduff, confirming suspicions which Macbeth claims to have had already. Now the play leads to their final meeting. Macduff shows that the witches' words concerning Macbeth's safety are useless, since they "palter . . . in a double sense". "None of woman born" seemed to mean "nobody at all"; but in another sense it means "no child to whom a woman has given natural birth". Macduff tells Macbeth that his mother did not "bear" him (in this second sense), and they fight until Macbeth is killed. Macduff leaves and returns after a moment with Macbeth's head carried in triumph.

Macduff represents the main opposition to Macbeth. He is the chief instrument by which Malcolm is able to obtain the throne of his father Duncan, and he everywhere acts with good sense, bravery and nobleness of nature. Only his wife doubts the wisdom of his flight to England, calling it "madness", and a mixture of fear and treachery. She accuses him too of lacking "the natural touch", the quality of humanity, but, when told of the murder of his family, he says simply,

> I must . . . feel it as a man (IV.iii.221).

If Macbeth's ambitions had had good ends, not evil ones, his wife *Lady Macbeth* would have been the perfect partner for him, for she completes his personality, and provides just those qualities which he lacks. If the play is complete in the form in which we now know it, there exists an understanding between Macbeth and his wife which depends on feelings rather than words. For when we first see Lady Macbeth, she is reading a letter from her husband telling her of the witches' prophecy and particularly that he is, according to that prophecy, destined to become king. She, too, is intensely ambitious, and cannot bear even to mention the kingship directly; she can say only:

> thou . . . shalt be
> What thou art promised (I.v.13–14).

But she is afraid that he is not evil enough to obtain it by the most direct means. She reveals her own nature most fully in the address she then makes to the spirits of evil:

> Come, you spirits
> That tend on mortal thoughts, unsex me here,
> And fill me, from the crown to the toe, top-full
> Of direst cruelty! . . . (I.v.38–41).

Realizing that her husband's hopes of the crown may be impeded by his feelings of humanity, she prays that her own similar feelings may be suppressed. This proves that she is not the hard, cold, unfeeling villain of the piece, but one who, if she is to attain what she aims at, will also have to reckon with those finer feelings which are common to most human natures. But she is, perhaps, more purposeful, less ready to consider secondary matters (even those which concern conscience), and this is why she, unlike her husband, has no need of supernatural encouragement, and therefore why none is given to her.

When her husband comes soon after her first appearance, they understand one another exactly, Without saying so, each realizes that Duncan will not leave the castle alive. Lady Macbeth seems to wish that the whole plan should be put into her hands, for she thinks she is now supremely firm in her purpose. But when the time is right for the murder, and she has urged Macbeth's purpose to the utmost, she shows that she too has had uneasy feelings; for, as the noise of Macbeth calling out at the back suggests that he has been discovered and has failed in his attempt, she admits that she could not have done the deed herself:

> Had he not resembled
> My father as he slept, I had done 't (II.ii.12–13).

However, even if her actions are hindered, she thinks quickly. Her impassioned speeches when Macbeth first comes to her in the play are in significant contrast to those in which she smoothly and humbly flatters her guest Duncan with her offers of service. And so it is through the play; Macbeth is again and again relieved of burdens and accusations because his wife is ready to excuse him and explain away what seems so evil. When Macbeth has murdered Duncan he is haunted with the vision of murderous hands turned against him. His wife is not so troubled, and when the knocking begins at the outer gate she is ready with measures to conceal the crime. She sees the blood on his hands, and says,

> A little water clears us of this deed (II.ii.66);

and she realizes that they must quickly get on their night-clothes or people will wonder why they were not in bed when Duncan was murdered. And when, after the discovery of the murder, Macduff asks Macbeth why he murdered Duncan's attendants and Macbeth's answer is too sensational to be very convincing, his wife quickly notices it, and pretends to faint so that attention is distracted from her husband.

For the murder of Banquo, Macbeth seems at first to be less dependent upon his wife. It is he who plans it with the two murderers, and then tells his wife about it. She is at first unsure, but is soon convinced, and then Macbeth plays the lordly husband:

> Be innocent of the knowledge, dearest chuck,
> Till thou applaud the deed (III.ii.46–7).

He cannot know how soon he will once more need to depend upon her. Banquo's ghost comes to haunt his state banquet; Lady Macbeth again quickly understands what is happening, though only her husband can see the ghost, and she tries to explain it away:

> Sit, worthy friends. My lord is often thus,
> And hath been from his youth (III.iv.53–4).

At the second appearance she speaks of her husband's fit as "a thing of custom", and even hints at a treatment for it:

> I pray you, speak not; he grows worse and worse;
> Question enrages him (III.iv.117–18)

—still as if the incident were a common one. She really thinks he needs sleep, and as soon as the guests have left in confusion and they have both mentioned Macduff as the next centre of opposition, Macbeth tries to rest.

Lady Macbeth, however, is unable to sleep in peace. In the great scene at the beginning of Act V she appears with a taper in her hand, walking in her sleep and reliving her experience and thoughts at the murder of Duncan. Again she speaks words of encouragement to her husband; she speaks her thoughts on the old man's bleeding, but mostly she thinks of the blood on her own hands which no water has been able to wash off:

> all the perfumes of Arabia will not sweeten this little hand
> (v.i.40–1).

This reveals without doubt who is responsible for the crimes, and shows that Lady Macbeth is no more able to free herself from conscience than her husband is.

She is not seen again. A cry of women is heard when Macbeth is putting in order the defences of his castle so as to be ready to face a siege, and this cry announces her death. She, too, has been unable to sleep, and her mind has become disturbed. (Malcolm and others believe that she took her own life; see v.ix.35–7.) To Macbeth, when he hears the news, life seems puzzling and without value. He has lost his best support and from now on he must fight alone.

Lady Macduff plays a small but much-loved part in the tragedy, since in a world of evil she and her son represent confused and lovable simplicity. Her husband has left her, she does not know why. Rosse tries to explain that Macduff has fled for his country's good, but Lady Macduff is unconvinced, and bitterly grieved:

> All is the fear, and nothing is the love;
> As little is the wisdom, where the flight
> So runs against all reason (iv.ii.12–14).

Rosse himself does not seem to be really convinced, and is near to tears. He leaves and there is an exchange between Lady Macduff and her son in which the tragedy of the situation is heightened by what at first seems artful word-play on the subject of husbands and fathers, although this is really a cover to feelings of tender love. The confusion reaches its height when Macbeth's agents murder Lady Macduff, although she has done no harm.

The Witches represent the most important supernatural element of the play, but "witch" is not a good word to denote them, for they are much more powerful and more evil than the simple, stupid old women who as "witches" were supposed by some to do harm to individuals through the use of magic powers. The word *witch* is, in fact, used only once in *Macbeth* (other than in the stage directions): the sailor's wife mentioned by the first witch (I.iii.4ff.) called her "witch" and was evidently severely punished for it. Elsewhere the women are called "the weird sisters", i.e. the sisters of fate. But even this title is inadequate, since, whatever they claim to have done to their other victims, they do not bring fate to Macbeth. Instead they try to persuade him to do wrong, or invite him to do it by deliberately deceiving him about what the future will hold. They embody evil and give to evil the respect which normal human beings give to good; they chant together "Fair is foul, and foul is fair" at the end of the first scene. For Macbeth they represent the bad forces struggling for his soul; his conscience warns him against them, and, knowing they are evil, he is free to make a choice. They win him by word-play, which is one form of deception.

To Banquo, who is less inclined than Macbeth to ignoble ambitions, they are content to prophesy, and their prophecies are favourable; his children are to be kings even though Macbeth, not he, will win the throne. To Macbeth they give some much-needed encouragement; in IV.i, he demands to know what they are doing, perhaps in order to find out if their influence can be turned to good account. In reply they bring up apparitions which foretell the future. The first warns him that Macduff will be a source of trouble to him; the second and third deceive him with hopeful prophecies which prove false. But he knows all the time that he is dealing with evil forces, for before his last visit to the weird sisters he tells his wife:

> I am bent to know,
> By the worst means, the worst (III.iv.134–5).

And he lives long enough to see how bad they were. When Birnam wood appears to move, something which seemed an impossibility, he begins

> To doubt th' equivocation of the fiend,
> That lies like truth (V.v.43–4),

for it seems that the weird sisters have sold their souls to the fiend, the devil. When Macduff says that he was not born of woman,

xxvii

Macbeth knows for sure that he has put his faith in evil, and has been betrayed:

> be these juggling fiends no more believed,
> That palter with us in a double sense,
> That keep the word of promise to our ear,
> And break it to our hope (v.viii.19–22).

(Act III, Scene v, shows the witches as different in some ways from this description of the part they play in the rest of the tragedy; but this scene is generally considered not to be part of the original play. See p. 134, n. 13.)

NOTE ON THE ILLUSTRATIONS

In the third edition line illustrations have been included. These illustrations, apart from being attractive in themselves, are intended to clarify difficulties in the text and have all been selected and prepared with this aim in mind. Where possible they are based on contemporary sources.

DRAMATIS PERSONAE

DUNCAN, *King of Scotland*
MALCOLM ⎫
DONALBAIN ⎭ *the King's sons*
MACBETH ⎫
BANQUO ⎭ *Generals of the King's Army*
MACDUFF ⎫
LENOX ⎪
ROSSE ⎪
MENTETH ⎬ *Noblemen of Scotland*
ANGUS ⎪
CATHNESS ⎭
FLEANCE, *Banquo's son*
SIWARD, *Earl of Northumberland, General of the English Forces*
YOUNG SIWARD, *Siward's son*
SEYTON, *an officer, attending Macbeth*
BOY, *Macduff's son*
AN ENGLISH DOCTOR
A SCOTTISH DOCTOR
A SOLDIER
A PORTER
AN OLD MAN

LADY MACBETH
LADY MACDUFF
GENTLEWOMAN, *attending Lady Macbeth*
HECATE
THREE WITCHES

LORDS, GENTLEMEN, OFFICERS, SOLDIERS, MURDERERS,
  ATTENDANTS, AND MESSENGERS
THE GHOST OF BANQUO, AND OTHER APPARITIONS

The scenes are laid in Scotland, with the exception of IV.iii, *which takes place in England.*

(1.i) Three witches are speaking, amid thunder and lightning, while a battle is in progress. They arrange to meet Macbeth when the fight is over.

1 *When the hurlyburly 's done.* The witches propose to meet again when the battle now in progress is finished – when it is *lost and won* (line 4), i.e. lost by one side and therefore won by the other.

2 *ere the set of sun* – "before sunset".

3 *Graymalkin* is the name of a cat; witches were said to keep cats as assistants in their ceremonies.

4 *Paddock* – "toad".

5 *Anon!* – "(We are coming) at once!"

6 *Fair is foul, and foul is fair.* The good and bad are confused; there is an evil influence.

Of Kernes and Gallowglasses is supplied[12]

MACBETH

ACT ONE

Scene I. An open place.
Thunder and lightning. Enter THREE WITCHES.

I WITCH

When shall we three meet again,
In thunder, lightning or in rain?

2 WITCH

When the hurlyburly 's done,[1]
When the battle 's lost and won.

3 WITCH

That will be ere the set of sun.[2]   5

I WITCH

Where the place?

2 WITCH

Upon the heath.

3 WITCH

There to meet with Macbeth.

I WITCH

I come, Graymalkin![3]

ALL

Paddock[4] calls. —,Anon![5] —
Fair is foul, and foul is fair:[6]   10
Hover through the fog and filthy air.

[*Exeunt*

2—M.

(I.ii) King Duncan, with his sons Malcolm and Donalbain, meet a wounded officer who has just come from the battle. The fight is between the Scottish forces, in which Duncan's kinsman Macbeth has high command, and a rebel army under Macdonwald. With the rebel army is the king of Norway and a fresh body of his men who have helped to make possible a further attack; but Macdonwald has been killed. As the officer is taken out, Rosse enters with later news: the king of Norway and another rebel nobleman, the Thane of Cawdor, have been defeated.

1 *Alarm within.* A trumpet call sounds from the back of the stage to show that the king is entering. The camp is the base of the Scottish forces, and we are able to follow the course of the battle by hearing what various speakers have to say about it.

2 *He can report . . . newest state* – "He can tell us, as it seems by his sad condition (for he is bleeding badly), the latest state of the battle"; *newest* – "most recent".

3 *sergeant.* The soldier is called a captain in the stage direction and a sergeant here; he is certainly a full officer.

4 *fought 'Gainst my captivity* – "fought against them (the enemy) when they were trying to capture me".

5 *Say to* – "Tell".

6 *knowledge* – "what you know".

7 *Doubtful it stood* – "It stood in doubt", i.e. undecided as to which side would win.

8 *As two spent swimmers . . . their art* – "like two swimmers weak through tiredness (*spent*), who hold each other tightly and prevent each other from using their skill (*art*) in swimming".

9 *Macdonwald*, a Scotsman fighting on the side of the Norwegians.

10 *Worthy to be a rebel* – "deserving the name rebel".

11 *for to that . . . swarm upon him* – "for to that extent (i.e. the extent of being a rebel) the great number of wicked deeds in man's nature are settled on him". The words *multiplying* and *swarm* suggest a cloud of horrible insects settled together in one place.

12 *. . . from the western isles . . . supplied.* Macdonwald (line 9) "is supported by light-armed Irish foot-soldiers (*Kernes*) and heavy-armed retainers (*Gallowglasses*) from the western isles". These *western isles* are the islands west of Scotland, i.e. the Hebrides and Ireland (see illustration p. xxx).

13 *And Fortune . . . rebel's whore* – "Fortune, who smiled on his wicked (*damnèd*) fighting, showed herself to be like a mistress (*whore*) in the company of a rebel". She acted like a bad woman, smiling but not loving; it looked as if the rebel forces were winning, but they were not.

14 *all's too weak* – "all (Macdonwald's efforts) were not strong enough (to fight against Macbeth's forces)".

15 *that name*, i.e. being called *brave*.

16 *steel* – "sword".

17 *smoked with bloody execution; execution* – "killing". The blood on Macbeth's sword was so fresh that it was still warm, and vapour rose from it; it *smoked*.

18 *Like Valour's minion* – "like the special favourite of Valour".

19 *carved out his passage* – "cut a way for himself (through the enemy forces)".

20 *Till he faced the slave* – "until he stood face to face with the wicked man (*slave*)". The general sense of this passage (lines 16–20) is: Scorning the help of Fortune, brave Macbeth, like the favourite of Valour, cut a way for himself with his drawn sword, which "smoked" with fresh blood, until he stood face to face with the villain Macdonwald.

Scene II. A camp near Forres.

Alarm within.[1] *Enter* KING DUNCAN,
MALCOLM, DONALBAIN, LENOX,
with Attendants, *meeting a bleeding* CAPTAIN.

DUNCAN

[*To the Lords*] What bloody man is that? He can report,
As seemeth by his plight, of the revolt
The newest state.[2]

MALCOLM

This is the sergeant[3]
Who, like a good and hardy soldier, fought
'Gainst my captivity.[4] – [*To the soldier*] Hail, brave friend!   5
Say to[5] the King the knowledge[6] of the broil,
As thou didst leave it.

CAPTAIN

Doubtful it stood,[7]
As two spent swimmers, that do cling together
And choke their art.[8] The merciless Macdonwald[9]
(Worthy to be a rebel,[10] for to that   10
The multiplying villainies of nature
Do swarm upon him)[11] from the western isles
Of Kernes and Gallowglasses is supplied;[12]
And Fortune, on his damnèd quarrel smiling,
Showed like a rebel's whore:[13] but all 's too weak;[14]   15
For brave Macbeth (well he deserves that name),[15]
Disdaining Fortune, with his brandished steel,[16]
Which smoked with bloody execution,[17]
Like Valour's minion,[18] carved out his passage,[19]
Till he faced the slave;[20]   20

3

21 *Which ne'er shook hands* – "who (i.e. Macbeth) did not shake hands (in farewell to Macdonwald)". The polite expression is meant to contrast with the grim action.

22 *Till he unseamed . . . the chaps* – "until Macbeth had cut his body open". Macbeth "opened a seam" in his skin from the navel (*nave*) to the jaw (*chaps*).

23 *And fixed his head . . . battlements.* Defeated rebels were beheaded, and their heads displayed on the walls of a castle as a warning to others (see illustration p. 6).

24 *As whence* (line 25) *. . . Discomfort swells* – "just as ship-wrecking storms and terrible (*direful*) thunder break out from the place where the sun begins to shine, so trouble comes (*Discomfort swells*) from the source (*spring*) that seemed to be giving relief (*comfort*)." When everything seems to be going well after some trouble, a set-back may be expected; the Captain goes on to say (lines 29–33) that in this way the Norwegian army, after its apparent defeat, was reinforced and it then attacked again.

25 *Mark* – "Notice".

26 *No sooner justice . . . armed*; *justice* and *valour* both refer to the Scottish forces – they are fighting in a just cause, and bravely.

27 *to trust their heels* – "to run away (to save their lives)".

28 *But* – "than", continuing the idea begun by *No sooner* (line 29).

29 *surveying vantage* – "seeing that they were in a good position".

30 *Yes; As sparrows . . . lion.* The new attack worried Macbeth and Banquo as much as sparrows worry eagles, or hares worry lions, i.e. not at all.

31 *they*, i.e. Macbeth and Banquo.

32 *As cannons . . . double cracks* – "like cannons full of extra-strong explosive" (see illustration p. 8).

33 *Except* – "if . . . not": "If they did not mean to *bathe* in their (the enemy's) reeking wounds, or celebrate (*memorise*) another Golgotha, I cannot tell . . ." The Captain is too weak from his own wounds to finish the sentence; he must be intending to say that he cannot tell what it was they aimed at, their bravery being so great. *Golgotha* is the place where Jesus was put to death.

34 *So well . . . wounds* – "Your words speak as well of you as your wounds do".

35 *smack of* – "taste of", and therefore "indicate"; "both of these things (i.e. the Captain's words and his wounds) indicate honour".

4

Which ne'er shook hands,[21] nor bade farewell to him,
Till he unseamed him from the nave to the chaps,[22]
And fixed his head upon our battlements.[23]

DUNCAN

O valiant cousin! worthy gentleman!

CAPTAIN

As whence the sun 'gins his reflection,   25
Shipwracking storms and direful thunders break,
So from that spring, whence comfort seemed to come,
Discomfort swells.[24] Mark,[25] King of Scotland, mark:
No sooner justice had, with valour armed,[26]
Compelled these skipping Kernes to trust their heels,[27]   30
But[28] the Norweyan lord, surveying vantage,[29]
With furbished arms, and new supplies of men,
Began a fresh assault.

DUNCAN

                    Dismayed not this
Our captains, Macbeth and Banquo?

CAPTAIN

                         Yes;
As sparrows eagles, or the hare the lion.[30]   35
If I say sooth, I must report they[31] were
As cannons overcharged with double cracks;[32]
So they
Doubly redoubled strokes upon the foe:
Except[33] they meant to bathe in reeking wounds,   40
Or memorise another Golgotha,
I cannot tell –
But I am faint; my gashes cry for help.

DUNCAN

So well thy words become thee, as thy wounds:[34]
They smack of[35] honour both. – Go, get him surgeons.   45
                         [*Exit* CAPTAIN, *attended*

5

36 *What a haste . . . his eyes!* – "The look in his eyes shows that he is in a great hurry!" "How hurried he looks!"

37 *So should . . . things strange* – "A man who is going to tell strange things would look like this"; *he* – "someone, a man".

38 *God save the King!* – "May God save the King", a greeting.

39 *Where the Norweyan . . . people cold.* – "where the Norwegian (*Norweyan*) flags mock (*flout*) the sky, and fan our people cold". This was the situation before Macbeth entered the fight; the Norwegian flags mocked the Scottish sky, and turned the people cold with fear (see illustration p. 10).

40 *Norway*, i.e. the king of Norway.

41 *numbers* of men.

42 *dismal* – "terrible".

43 *that Bellona's bridegroom* is Macbeth, represented as having "married" the Roman goddess of war, and therefore as being a great soldier.

44 *lapped in proof* – "clothed (wrapped up) in good (*proved*) armour".

45 *self-comparisons* – "equality with himself", i.e. a man as fine (in skill and courage) as he was.

46 *Point* is used for sword; "(his) sword against his enemy's".

47 *lavish* – "over-full (of insulting behaviour)".

48 *That* – "so that . . ." (he is continuing the story).

49 *craves composition* – "asks for terms (of peace)".

And fixed his head upon our battlements[23]

6

Enter ROSSE *and* ANGUS

[*Turning*] Who comes here?

MALCOLM

The worthy Thane of Rosse.

LENOX

What a haste looks through his eyes![36]
So should he look that seems to speak things strange.[37]

ROSSE

God save the King![38]

DUNCAN

Whence camest thou, worthy thane?

ROSSE

From Fife, great King,   50
Where the Norweyan banners flout the sky
And fan our people cold.[39]
Norway[40] himself, with terrible numbers,[41]
Assisted by that most disloyal traitor,
The Thane of Cawdor, began a dismal[42] conflict;   55
Till that Bellona's bridegroom,[43] lapped in proof,[44]
Confronted him with self-comparisons,[45]
Point[46] against point, rebellious arm 'gainst arm,
Curbing his lavish[47] spirit: and, to conclude,
The victory fell on us; –

DUNCAN

Great happiness!   60

ROSSE

That[48] now
Sweno, the Norways' king, craves composition;[49]

50 *Nor would we . . . his men* – "and we refused to allow him to bury his men . . ."

51 *Saint Colmè's Inch* (now called Inchcolm) is a small island near Edinburgh, off the coast of Scotland. The name means "St. Columba's Island".

52 *to our general use*, i.e. for the use of all, not just for the king alone.

53 *No more . . . shall deceive* – "That Thane of Cawdor shall no longer (*no more*) deceive . . ."

54 *Our bosom interest* – "the interest I have close at heart". The king often refers to himself as *we*, not *I*, but the words *bosom interest* show that he is speaking of himself, contrasting with the *general use* in line 65.

55 *pronounce* – "make known".

56 *present* – "immediate"; he must die at once.

57 *with his former title greet Macbeth* – "greet Macbeth with the title which used to be the Thane of Cawdor's (i.e. *Thane of Cawdor*)". When a thane died his title was given to someone else, often, though not in this case, a close relative.

(I.iii) The three witches meet again, and tell each other what they have been doing and intend to do. Then Macbeth, with Banquo at his side, comes upon them by surprise. They greet Macbeth as Thane of Glamis, Thane of Cawdor and "king hereafter". Banquo, they say, will never be king himself, but will be father to a line of kings. Macbeth is already Thane of Glamis, and he believes that the Thane of Cawdor is still alive. But Rosse and Angus come to tell him that the present Cawdor is under sentence of death and that the King has given his title to Macbeth. Then Macbeth's thoughts turn to the kingship, and he wonders by what means he may obtain it.

1 The witches are now meeting again, as they said they would at the beginning of the play.

2 *A sailor's wife*, i.e. a woman she met.

3 "*Give me*" – "Give me some (of your chestnuts)".

As cannons overcharged with double cracks[32]

8

Nor would we deign him burial of his men[50]
Till he disbursèd at Saint Colmè's Inch[51]
Ten thousand dollars to our general use.[52]   65

DUNCAN

No more that Thane of Cawdor shall deceive[53]
Our bosom interest.[54] – Go, pronounce[55] his present[56] death,
And with his former title greet Macbeth.[57]

ROSSE

I 'll see it done.

DUNCAN

What he hath lost, noble Macbeth hath won.   70

[*Exeunt*

Scene III. *A heath.*

Thunder. Enter THREE WITCHES.[1]

1 WITCH

Where hast thou been, sister?

2 WITCH

Killing swine.

3 WITCH

Sister, where thou?

1 WITCH

A sailor's wife[2] had chestnuts in her lap,
And munched, and munched, and munched: "Give me,"[3]
    quoth I: 5

4 *Aroint* – "Go away!" As the sailor's wife refused to give any chestnuts to the witch, she curses the sailor husband – he has gone to Aleppo, but she will follow him even there.

5 *rump-fed ronyon* – foul fat woman.

6 His ship is called the *Tiger*.

7 *in a sieve*. The witch plans to sail in a sieve, which, being full of holes, would not make a boat for an ordinary human being.

8 *a rat without a tail*. Witches could change themselves into animals, it was believed, but no part of their bodies could become a tail.

9 *I'll do*. As a rat, she will eat away the side of the ship, piece by piece.

10 *I'll give thee a wind*. Witches were supposed to "sell" winds.

11 *the other* – "the others", the other winds.

12 *And the very . . . blow* – "and even the ports which the winds blow from", keeping the ships away.

13 *the quarters . . . I' the shipman's card* are the points of the seaman's compass.

14 *his penthouse lid* – "eyelid", which looks like the roof over a small building (*penthouse*).

15 *forbid* (for *forbidden*) – "cursed".

16 *sev'n-nights* – "weeks" (compare *fortnight* – "fourteen nights").

17 *peak and pine* – "waste away with suffering". He shall not be able to sleep even though "for a very long time (*nine times nine* weeks) he shall be tired, and waste away with suffering".

18 *tempest-tost* – "tossed by tempests".

banners flout the sky[39]

10

"Aroint[4] thee, witch!" the rump-fed ronyon[5] cries.
Her husband 's to Aleppo gone, master o' the Tiger:[6]
But in a sieve[7] I 'll thither sail,
And, like a rat without a tail,[8]
I 'll do,[9] I 'll do, and I 'll do.   10

2 WITCH

I 'll give thee a wind.[10]

1 WITCH

Th' art kind.

3 WITCH

And I another.

1 WITCH

I myself have all the other;[11]
And the very ports they blow,[12]   15
All the quarters that they know
I' the shipman's card;[13]
I 'll drain him dry as hay:
Sleep shall neither night nor day
Hang upon his penthouse lid;[14]   20
He shall live a man forbid.[15]
Weary sev'n-nights[16] nine times nine,
Shall he dwindle, peak and pine:[17]
Though his bark cannot be lost,
Yet it shall be tempest-tost.[18]   25
Look what I have.

2 WITCH

Show me, show me.

1 WITCH

Here I have a pilot's thumb,

11

19 *within*, i.e. at the back of the stage.
20 *The weird sisters* – "The sisters of fate", the witches.
21 *Posters* – "people who travel quickly".
22 *Thus do go about, about* – "go like this, round and round".
23 *Thrice to thine . . . mine* – "Three times to your side, and three times to mine"; these must be figures in the dance.
24 *the charm 's wound up* – "the charm is ready for action".
25 *So foul . . . not seen* – "I have never seen a day so good and bad", good, because the battle has been won, bad with the thunder of the witches'

weather. The witches have already brought *fair* and *foul* together (1.i.9).
26 *How far is 't called . . .* – "How far do people say it is . . ."
27 *That look not* – "that they do not look".
28 *are you aught . . . question?* – "are you anything (*aught*) a man can talk to?" Their appearance is so strange that Banquo is at first unable to decide whether they are human or not.
29 *her choppy finger laying* – "laying her rough (*choppy*) finger".
30 *forbid me to interpret* – "prevent me from concluding".

his bark

Wrecked, as homeward he did come.   [*Drum within*[19]

3 WITCH

A drum! a drum!   30
Macbeth doth come.

ALL

The weird sisters,[20] hand in hand,
Posters[21] of the sea and land,
Thus do go about, about:[22]
Thrice to thine, and thrice to mine,[23]   35
And thrice again, to make up nine.
Peace! – the charm 's wound up.[24]

Enter MACBETH *and* BANQUO

MACBETH

So foul and fair a day I have not seen.[25]

BANQUO

How far is 't called[26] to Forres? – [*He notices the* WITCHES]
    What are these,
So withered and so wild in their attire   40
That look not[27] like th' inhabitants o' the earth
And yet are on 't? – [*He speaks to the* WITCHES] Live you? or
    are you aught
That man may question?[28] You seem to understand me,
By each at once her choppy finger laying[29]
Upon her skinny lips: you should be women,   45
And yet your beards forbid me to interpret[30]
That you are so.

MACBETH

Speak, if you can: – what are you?

13

31 *All hail* is a very honourable greeting. The witches address Macbeth, each giving him a kind of title: one calls him Thane of Glamis, the second Thane of Cawdor, and the third tells him he will become king of Scotland. The audience knows that Macbeth has already been made Thane of Cawdor by the king, but Macbeth himself does not.

32 *fantastical* – "something which exists only in the world of the imagination".

33 *show* – "appear to be".

34 *My noble partner* (line 54) . . . *rapt withal* – "You greet my noble partner with an honour which he already has (*present grace*: the First Witch called him Thane of Glamis); you predict great and noble possessions for him (*noble having*: the Second Witch called him Thane of Cawdor) and the expectation of becoming king (*royal hope*) – so that he seems buried in thought with it (*withal*)".

35 *beg nor fear . . . hate* – "who neither beg your favours nor fear your hate".

I WITCH

All hail,[31] Macbeth! hail to thee, Thane of Glamis!

2 WITCH

All hail, Macbeth! hail to thee, Thane of Cawdor!

3 WITCH

All hail, Macbeth! that shalt be king hereafter.   50

BANQUO

[*Turning to* MACBETH] Good Sir, why do you start, and seem to
  fear
Things that do sound so fair? – [*To the* WITCHES] I' the name of
  truth,
Are ye fantastical,[32] or that indeed
Which outwardly ye show?[33] My noble partner
You greet with present grace, and great prediction   55
Of noble having and of royal hope,
That he seems rapt withal:[34] to me you speak not.
If you can look into the seeds of time,
And say which grain will grow, and which will not,
Speak then to me, who neither beg nor fear   60
Your favours nor your hate.[35]

I WITCH

Hail!

2 WITCH

Hail!

3 WITCH

Hail!

I WITCH

Lesser than Macbeth, and greater.   65

36 *get* – "beget, be the father of".

37 *though thou be none* – "even though you are not to be one yourself".

38 *imperfect* in that they have answered imperfectly, without making their meaning clear.

39 *Sinel* was the name of the former Thane of Glamis. When a thane died or was displaced, a new thane of the same name was appointed; and one man could hold the thanage of more than one place, thus having a number of titles.

40 *Say, from whence . . . intelligence* – "Tell me from where you have this strange news".

41 *charge* – "order". But the witches will not be ordered, and disappear.

42 *these are of them* – "these (witches) are made of them".

43 *corporal* – "corporeal, having a body".

44 *Would they had stayed!* – "I wish they had stayed".

45 *Were such things . . . speak about* – "Were such things here as we are speaking about?"

46 *have we eaten . . . prisoner?* – "Have we been eating the root that makes one mad (*the insane root*), that makes a prisoner of one's reason?" The words suggest that Shakespeare had a particular root in mind; perhaps it was henbane.

Thane

2 WITCH

Not so happy, yet much happier.

3 WITCH

Thou shalt get[36] kings, though thou be none:[37]
So all hail, Macbeth and Banquo!

1 WITCH

Banquo and Macbeth, all hail!

MACBETH

Stay, you imperfect[38] speakers, tell me more.   70
By Sinel's[39] death, I know I am Thane of Glamis;
But how of Cawdor? the Thane of Cawdor lives,
A prosperous gentleman; and to be king
Stands not within the prospect of belief
No more than to be Cawdor. Say, from whence   75
You owe this strange intelligence?[40] or why
Upon this blasted heath you stop our way
With such prophetic greeting? Speak, I charge[41] you.
                              [WITCHES *vanish*

BANQUO

The earth hath bubbles, as the water has,
And these are of them.[42] – Whither are they vanished?   80

MACBETH

Into the air; and what seemed corporal,[43] melted
As breath into the wind. – Would they had stayed![44]

BANQUO

Were such things here, as we do speak about,[45]
Or have we eaten on the insane root
That takes the reason prisoner?[46]   85

17

47 *went it not so?* – "is that not what they said?"; *it* here suggests a melody – we might say, in Modern English, "I heard a beautiful melody yesterday. This is how it went." Banquo takes up the image in the following line.

48 *selfsame* – "just the same".

49 *His wonders . . . or his* – "his wonder (at your deeds) and his desire to praise you are both so strong in him that they fight one another (*contend*), so that he does not know which to express to you (*which should be thine*) and which to keep to himself (*or his*)". So he is silent.

50 *viewing o'er* – "looking over".

51 *Nothing afeard* – "not at all frightened". Macbeth killed many soldiers in the battle, making many *strange images of death* (line 97), but he was in no way frightened at them.

52 *As thick . . . with post* – "Messenger (*post*) after messenger ran (to us), as thick as hail".

53 *Thy praises . . . defence* – "praises of you (for what you did in) the great defence of this kingdom".

18

MACBETH

Your children shall be kings.

BANQUO

You shall be king.

MACBETH

And Thane of Cawdor too; went it not so?[47]

BANQUO

To the selfsame[48] tune and words. Who's here?

Enter ROSSE *and* ANGUS

ROSSE

The king hath happily received, Macbeth,
The news of thy success; and, when he reads   90
Thy personal venture in the rebels' fight,
His wonders and his praises do contend,
Which should be thine, or his.[49] Silenced with that,
In viewing o'er[50] the rest o' the selfsame day,
He finds thee in the stout Norweyan ranks,   95
Nothing afeard[51] of what thyself didst make,
Strange images of death. As thick as hail
Ran post with post;[52] and every one did bear
Thy praises in his kingdom's great defence,[53]
And poured them down before him.

ANGUS

                                        We are sent   100
To give thee, from our royal master, thanks;
Only to herald thee into his sight,
Not pay thee.

19

ACT ONE

54 *for an earnest*. An *earnest* is a payment
put down to fix a bargain. The
lordship of Cawdor is said to be an
honour which is simply a reward
promising further honours.

55 *call thee* – "give you the title of".

56 *addition* – "title", i.e. a name *added*
to those given at birth.

57 *borrowed robes*. The robes are poetic
symbols of the honours they show.
Borrowed robes are other people's
honours, which he has no right to
wear.

58 *Who was* – "The man who was . . ."

59 *But under heavy . . . deserves to lose* –
"he is still living, but under sentence of death (*heavy judgement*), as
he deserves".

60 *combined With those of Norway* –
"joined with the Norwegian
forces".

61 *line* – "strengthen", as cloth is
strengthened with a lining.

62 *hidden* – "secret".

63 *both*, i.e. open co-operation and
secret help.

64 *treasons capital* – "acts of treason
which are punishable by death".

65 *The greatest is behind* – "the greatest
(honour) is following, still to
come", i.e. the honour of being
king.

66 *pains* – "trouble".

67 *Thane* – "title of Thane".

68 *no less*, i.e. nothing less than kingship.

69 *trusted home* – "if believed right to
the end". (For the use of *home* here,
compare the Modern English "to
drive a nail home", i.e. right into
the wood.)

70 *enkindle you* – "set you on fire",
here with the idea of the burning
glory of kingship; and the crown,
the sign of kingship, "burns" with
shining gold. But fire also burns up,
as Macbeth might be burnt up by
his own ambition.

20

ROSSE

And, for an earnest[54] of a greater honour,
He bade me, from him, call thee[55] Thane of Cawdor: 105
In which addition,[56] Hail! most worthy thane,
For it is thine.

BANQUO

What! can the devil speak true?

MACBETH

The Thane of Cawdor lives: why do you dress me
In borrowed robes?[57]

ANGUS

                    Who was[58] the thane lives yet;
But under heavy judgement bears that life   110
Which he deserves to lose.[59] Whether he was combined
With those of Norway,[60] or did line[61] the rebel
With hidden[62] help and vantage, or that with both[63]
He laboured in his country's wrack, I know not;
But treasons capital,[64] confessed and proved,   115
Have overthrown him.

MACBETH

            [Aside] Glamis, and Thane of Cawdor:
The greatest is behind.[65]
[To ROSSE and ANGUS] Thanks for your pains.[66]
[To BANQUO] Do you not hope your children shall be kings,
When those that gave the Thane[67] of Cawdor to me
Promised no less[68] to them?

BANQUO

                    That, trusted home,[69]   120
Might yet enkindle you[70] unto the crown

21

71 *Besides* – "as well as".

72 *oftentimes* – "often".

73 *The instruments of darkness* – "unearthly powers", in this case the witches who "tell us what is true in order to do us harm". This train of thought continues in the next two lines (125–6): "(these powers) win us with what is unimportant (though true) in order to betray us in most important things".

74 *deepest consequence* – i.e. "(matters of) the gravest importance".

75 *a word, I pray you*. The news that Macbeth is now Thane of Cawdor sets him thinking, and these thoughts must be expressed, for they are necessary to the progress of the play. He must turn aside from the other characters on the stage, and this is arranged by Banquo calling his friends aside. Macbeth then speaks his thoughts unheard by the others.

76 *the swelling act . . . theme*. Macbeth here borrows terms from the theatre, and uses them to describe the witches' prophecy; *the swelling act* – "the part of the play in which a small event becomes something bigger"; *the imperial theme* – "the subject of empire", i.e. of the kingship of Scotland. The titles of Glamis and Cawdor are prologues to the main part of the play, that about the honour of being king.

77 *ill* – "bad".

78 *earnest* – "promise"; compare line 104 of this scene. Macbeth's argument is that the witches' words cannot be bad, or they would not have given him a promise of success by beginning with something that has actually become true (*Commencing in a truth*, line 133).

79 The *suggestion* is one which, as yet, exists only in his mind: it is the possibility of murdering King Duncan.

80 *unfix my hair* – "frighten me"; or, in the Modern English expression, "make my hair stand on end".

81 *seated heart . . . ribs*. The thought of murder makes his heart beat strongly; although it is fixed (*seated*) in his body, it beats against his ribs.

82 *Against the use* – "not according to the custom".

83 *My thought . . . fantastical* – "My thought, in which murder is, as yet, only an object of the imagination (*fantastical*)". In the early history of Scotland, the crown did not pass from father to son as a matter of course. Macbeth, a noble and popular figure, might himself succeed to the throne if the king should die. But Duncan has a son, and this son is later made heir apparent (I.iv.37–8).

84 *single* – "weak".

85 *function . . . surmise* – "action is kept down by imagination".

86 *nothing is . . . is not* – "nothing exists (for me) except that which has no existence"; he is speaking of his thoughts, which now engage all his powers.

87 *our partner 's rapt*. Macbeth is carried away by his thoughts to such an extent that even when Banquo draws attention to his state he does not hear him. Instead he follows the former course of his thoughts.

88 *Without my stir* – "without my doing anything (about it)". If Fate says he is to be king, he certainly will be, whether or not he takes any action to that end.

22

Besides[71] the Thane of Cawdor. But 't is strange:
And oftentimes,[72] to win us to our harm,
The instruments of darkness[73] tell us truths,
Win us with honest trifles, to betray 's   125
In deepest consequence.[74] — something small
[*To* ROSSE *and* ANGUS] Cousins, a word, I pray you.[75]

MACBETH

                    [*Aside*] Two truths are told
As happy prologues to the swelling act
Of the imperial theme.[76]
[*To* ROSSE *and* ANGUS] I thank you, gentlemen –
[*Aside*] This supernatural soliciting asking   130
Cannot be ill;[77] cannot be good: – if ill,
Why hath it given me earnest[78] of success,
Commencing in a truth? I am Thane of Cawdor:
If good, why do I yield to that suggestion[79]
Whose horrid image doth unfix my hair,[80]   135
And make my seated heart knock at my ribs[81]
Against the use[82] of nature? Present fears
Are less than horrible imaginings.
My thought, whose murder yet is but fantastical,[83]
Shakes so my single[84] state of man, that function   140
Is smothered in surmise,[85] and nothing is,
But what is not.[86]

BANQUO

[*To the Lords*] Look, how our partner 's rapt.[87] Lost

MACBETH

[*Aside*] If Chance will have me king, why, Chance may
    crown me,
Without my stir.[88]   paradoxical.

89 *our strange garments* – "clothes which are new and unfamiliar", and so do not fit very well until they have been used.

90 *the hour* – "the right hour (to do something)", the opportunity which will surely come however hard the day may be (*runs through the roughest day*).

91 *stay upon* – "wait for".

92 *Give me your favour* – "Excuse me".

93 *wrought* – "worried"; *overwrought* is used in Modern English for worry from too much excitement.

94 *your pains* (line 150) . . . *read them* – "your trouble is written down (as it were in a book) where every day I turn the page to read it"; i.e. "the trouble you have taken is always in my mind; I do not forget it".

95 *Let us* – "Let us go".

96 *Think upon* – "Think about".

97 *chanced* – "happened by chance".

98 *The interim . . . it* – "(we) having considered it in the time between now and then . . ."

99 *speak Our free hearts* – "talk openly".

BANQUO

New honours come upon him
Like our strange garments,[89] cleave not to their mould   145
But with the aid of use.

Stick
thy don't fit the body.

MACBETH

[*Aside*] Come what come may,
Time and the hour[90] runs through the roughest day.

BANQUO

Worthy Macbeth, we stay upon[91] your leisure.

MACBETH

[*To the Lords*] Give me your favour:[92] my dull brain was
    wrought[93]
With things forgotten. Kind gentlemen, your pains   150
Are registered where every day I turn
The leaf to read them.[94] – Let us[95] toward the king. –
[*To* BANQUO] Think upon[96] what hath chanced;[97] and at more
    time,
The interim having weighed it,[98] let us speak
Our free hearts[99] each to other.

BANQUO

Very gladly.   155

MACBETH

Till then, enough. – [*To All*] Come, friends.

[*Exeunt*

(I.iv) In the castle of Forres, Duncan asks his son whether Cawdor has already been executed; he is told that Cawdor confessed his treachery and died a noble death. Duncan observes how much appearances can deceive, and Macbeth (another deceiver, though Duncan does not know it) enters with the nobles. Duncan thanks him for the part he has played in the battle, and Macbeth professes it to be nothing but his duty to his king. Duncan proclaims Malcolm as his heir, and also Duke of Cumberland: Macbeth immediately sees this as a hindrance to his own ambitions, and he begins to think of evil ways to ensure that the witches' prophecy comes true.

1 *Is execution . . . Cawdor?* – "Has the Thane of Cawdor been executed (yet)?" Malcolm says he has heard so; and this scene then passes to further glorification of Macbeth, who is now Thane of Cawdor himself. There is one setback: Duncan appoints his son as his successor to the throne. How, then, shall Macbeth be king?

2 *in commission* – "with orders (to carry out the execution)". Angus knew that the thane was under sentence of death (I.iii.110).

3 *one* – "someone", not, of course, one of those with orders to execute Cawdor.

4 *very frankly* (line 5) . . . *deep repentance*. Notice that Cawdor, although a traitor, died honourably; this is another instance of the confusion between good and evil so characteristic of the play: "fair is foul and foul is fair".

5 *Nothing in his life . . . leaving it* – "Nothing in his life was so honourable to him as the way in which he left it", i.e. "the way he died".

6 *had been studied* – "had studied his part well", like an actor in the theatre.

7 *As 't were* – "as if it were".

8 *a careless trifle* – "a small thing, not worth caring about".

9 *There 's no art . . . in the face* – "There is no skill (*art*) by which one can find the construction of a person's mind in his face"; it is impossible to look into a person's face and know what he is thinking.

10 *even now* – "just now". He says he was worried because he had up to then had no opportunity of thanking Macbeth for his services. The way he says this is very formal and Macbeth takes up the formality from him.

11 *before* – "in front". The king is saying, in effect, that Macbeth is far ahead of them (in deeds), so that gratitude, however quickly given (*swiftest wing of recompense*), has difficulty in catching him up.

12 *would thou hadst* (line 18) . . . *been mine!* – "I wish you had deserved less (of me), so that I might have been able to give you the right amount (*proportion*) of both thanks and payment".

13 *only I . . . say* – "I have only this left to say (to you)".

14 *More is thy due . . . can pay* – "what you deserve is more than all of us can pay".

26

Scene IV. Forres. A room in the King's palace.
Flourish of trumpets. Enter DUNCAN, MALCOLM,
DONALBAIN, LENOX, *and* Attendants.

DUNCAN

Is execution done on Cawdor?[1] Are not
Those in commission[2] yet returned?

MALCOLM

          My liege,
They are not yet come back; but I have spoke
With one[3] that saw him die: who did report
That very frankly he confessed his treasons,   5
Implored your highness' pardon, and set forth
A deep repentance.[4] Nothing in his life
Became him like the leaving it:[5] he died
As one that had been studied[6] in his death,
To throw away the dearest thing he owed   10
As 't were[7] a careless trifle.[8]

DUNCAN

       There 's no art
To find the mind's construction in the face:[9]
He was a gentleman on whom I built
An absolute trust —

Enter MACBETH, BANQUO, ROSSE, *and* ANGUS.

  [*To* MACBETH] O worthiest cousin!
The sin of my ingratitude even now[10]   15
Was heavy on me. Thou art so far before,[11]
That swiftest wing of recompense is slow
To overtake thee: would thou hadst less deserved,
That the proportion both of thanks and payment
Might have been mine![12] only I have left to say:[13]   20
More is thy due than more than all can pay.[14]

15 *In doing it* – "by giving it" (i.e. the service and the loyalty).

16 *part* – "rôle", an actor's part on the stage.

17 *Safe toward* – "to safeguard".

18 *I have begun to plant thee* – the king is placing Macbeth in a position where his honour will "grow" or develop, like a plant set in the earth. The gardening metaphor is continued in the next line, *full of growing*, and Banquo takes it up in lines 32–3: *There if I grow, The harvest is your own.*

19 *labour* – "try hard".

20 *infold* – "embrace".

21 *There if I grow* – "if I grow there". This takes up the gardening metaphors in the last few lines.

22 *Wanton in fulness* – "so full as to be out of control".

23 *drops of sorrow* – "tears".

24 *the nearest*, i.e. "the nearest to me".

25 *We will establish . . . Malcolm* – "I will settle my estate on my eldest son Malcolm". The king is here making a public statement, and refers to himself as *we*, not *I*. And *estate* means not only lands and money but also title, here the title of king.

26 *which honour must* (line 39) . . . .*all deservers* – "this is not an honour for him alone; other honours (*signs of nobleness*) shall shine like stars on all who deserve them".

27 The castle at *Inverness* is Macbeth's home, and there the king proposes to visit him.

28 *bind us* – "make me indebted". By going to Inverness and staying at Macbeth's castle, the king is even more indebted to Macbeth for services.

MACBETH

The service and the loyalty I owe,
In doing it,[15] pays itself. Your highness' part[16]
Is to receive our duties: and our duties
Are, to your throne and state, children and servants;   25
Which do but what they should, by doing everything
Safe toward[17] your love and honour.

DUNCAN

Welcome hither:
I have begun to plant thee,[18] and will labour[19]
To make thee full of growing. [*To* BANQUO] – Noble
  Banquo,
That hast no less deserved, nor must be known   30
No less to have done so, let me infold[20] thee,
And hold thee to my heart.

BANQUO

There if I grow,[21]
The harvest is your own.

DUNCAN

My plenteous joys,
Wanton in fulness,[22] seek to hide themselves
In drops of sorrow.[23] – [*To All*] Sons, kinsmen, thanes,   35
And you whose places are the nearest,[24] know,
We will establish our estate upon
Our eldest, Malcolm;[25] whom we name hereafter
The Prince of Cumberland: which honour must
Not, unaccompanied, invest him only,   40
But signs of nobleness, like stars, shall shine
On all deservers.[26] – [*To* MACBETH] From hence to
  Inverness,[27]
And bind us[28] further to you.

29

29 *The rest . . . for you* – "Everything is labour except what is done in your service". *The rest* – "what remains, everything except . . ."

30 *harbinger* – "messenger", especially someone sent on ahead to arrange for the reception of an important visitor. It is very important to Macbeth's plans that he should get to his castle before the king arrives, so as to be able to tell his wife some of the ideas which are burning in his mind.

31 *your approach* – "your coming near (to my castle)".

32 As Macbeth now speaks to himself, he leaves the stiff, courtly style he has been using with the king, and speaks plainly; the prince stands in his way if he is to become king.

33 *a step.* This step lies in his way; he can jump over it, and then it will lead to something higher; or he can fall over it, and then all his plans are at an end.

34 *The eye wink at the hand* – "(let) the eye close for a moment and not see what the hand is doing".

35 While Macbeth has been speaking his thoughts aloud, Duncan and Banquo have been talking about him. They now come forward, and Duncan finishes the scene with a short speech.

36 *full so valiant* – "quite as brave (as you have just been saying)".

37 *And in his commendations . . . fed* – "I am fed full with good reports about him"; *banquet* in the following line continues the food metaphor.

38 *after him* – "follow him".

39 *Whose care . . . before* – "who has taken the trouble to go on in front . . ."

40 *It is a peerless kinsman* – "he is a relation without equal". Macbeth's mother and Duncan's mother were sisters.

(I.v) In Macbeth's castle at Inverness, Lady Macbeth reads a letter from her husband in which he tells her of his meeting with the witches. She begins to think of the coming struggle between his ambition and his humanity. A messenger announces that the king is on his way to Macbeth's castle, and Lady Macbeth is determined that he shall not leave it alive. In a moment her husband is with her and they agree on what is to be done.

1 *reading a letter.* This letter is from Macbeth; in it he tells his wife of the meeting with the witches, of the truth of what they foretold and of his hopes for the future.

2 *They*, i.e. the witches.

3 *perfect'st* – "most perfect".

4 *they have more . . . knowledge* – "the knowledge they have is more than mortal"; it is supernatural.

MACBETH

The rest is labour, which is not used for you:[29]
I 'll be myself the harbinger,[30] and make joyful   45
The hearing of my wife with your approach;[31]
So, humbly take my leave.

DUNCAN

My worthy Cawdor!

MACBETH

[*Aside*][32] The Prince of Cumberland! — That is a step[33]
On which I must fall down, or else o'erleap,
For in my way it lies. Stars, hide your fires!   50
Let not light see my black and deep desires;
The eye wink at the hand,[34] yet let that be,
Which the eye fears, when it is done, to see.

[*Exit*

DUNCAN

True, worthy Banquo,[35] he is full so valiant,[36]
And in his commendations I am fed;[37]   55
It is a banquet to me. Let 's after him,[38]
Whose care is gone before[39] to bid us welcome:
It is a peerless kinsman.[40]

[*Flourish. Exeunt*

Scene V. Inverness. A room in MACBETH'S *castle.*
Enter LADY MACBETH, *reading a letter.*[1]

LADY MACBETH

"They[2] met me in the day of success; and I have learnt by the
perfect'st[3] report, they have more in them than mortal knowledge.[4] When I burned in desire to question them further, they
made themselves air, into which they vanished. Whiles I stood

31

5 *missives* – "messengers".

6 *all-hailed* – "greeted with honour" (see I.iii.106).

7 *deliver thee* – "tell you about".

8 *dues of rejoicing* – "the rejoicing which is proper (at this happy news)".

9 *Lay it to thy heart* – "Think about it in secret". Notice how different Macbeth's style here is from that of his speeches of thanks and humility before the king. Here he is serious and direct; so much so that when he arrives later in the scene, his wife and he understand each other perfectly, although neither even mentions a definite plan.

10 *Yet do . . . nature.* Lady Macbeth is uncertain about her husband's character (his *nature*), fearing that it will not be purposeful enough to carry out the plan which she, too, is thinking of.

11 *To catch* – "to seize". The *nearest way* is the quickest way to kingship, i.e. murder.

12 *Thou wouldst be* – "You want to be".

13 *Art not* – "you are not".

14 *without . . . attend it* – "(you are) without the evil nature (*illness*) which should go with (*attend*) it".

15 *what thou . . . thou holily* – "what you wish for according to your ambitions (*highly*) you want to get honourably (*holily*)". Macbeth wants to win high honours for himself without using evil means to do so.

16 *thou 'dst have, great Glamis* (line 20) . . . *be undone* – "Great Glamis! You want to have (*a*) that thing which cries, 'You must act in *this* way if you are to get it' (i.e. the crown) and (*b*) that thing which you are more (*rather*) frightened of doing than wish should not be done (i.e. the murder)". He fears to do it but he wishes it done.

17 *Hie thee hither* – "Hurry here to me".

18 *That* – "so that".

19 *pour my spirits. . . . ear* – "say things into your ear which will stir you (to action)".

20 *And chastise with the valour* (line 25) . . . *crowned withal.* Lady Macbeth vows to talk bravely to her husband (*the valour of my tongue*) and so beat down (*chastise*) everything which stands in his way to kingship. In line 26, the *golden round* is the crown; *metaphysical aid* in the next line is supernatural help (i.e. the favour of the weird sisters). The whole passage may thus be turned into Modern English: "and (so that I may) beat down with brave words everything that keeps you back from the golden crown which fate and supernatural aid seem to be honouring you with".

21 Lady Macbeth has had just enough time to read the letter and decide her part in the drama of murder and crowning before a messenger enters with news that the king is coming. It is part of her plan that the king should be in her hands, and fate has worked quickly to this end.

22 *tidings* – "news".

23 *thy master* – the messenger's master, Macbeth.

24 *were 't so* – "if it were so".

25 *Would have . . . preparation* – "would have sent news about it so that preparations could be made".

rapt in the wonder of it, came missives[5] from the king, who   5
all-hailed[6] me 'Thane of Cawdor'; by which title, before, these
weird sisters saluted me, and referred me to the coming-on of
time, with 'Hail, king that shalt be!' This have I thought good
to deliver thee,[7] my dearest partner of greatness, that thou
might'st not lose the dues of rejoicing,[8] by being ignorant   10
of what greatness is promised thee. Lay it to thy heart,[9] and
farewell."
Glamis thou art, and Cawdor; and shalt be
What thou art promised. – Yet do I fear thy nature:[10]
It is too full o' the milk of human kindness   15
To catch[11] the nearest way. Thou wouldst be[12] great;
Art not[13] without ambition, but without
The illness should attend it:[14] what thou wouldst highly,
That wouldst thou holily;[15] wouldst not play false,
And yet wouldst wrongly win; thou 'dst have, great Glamis, 20
That which cries, "Thus thou must do, if thou have it";
And that which rather thou dost fear to do,
Than wishest should be undone.[16] Hie thee hither,[17]
That[18] I may pour my spirits in thine ear,[19]
And chastise with the valour of my tongue   25
All that impedes thee from the golden round,
Which fate and metaphysical aid doth seem
To have thee crowned withal.[20] –

Enter a Messenger[21]

What is your tidings?[22]

MESSENGER

The king comes here tonight.

LADY MACBETH

Thou 'rt mad to say it.
Is not thy master[23] with him? who, were 't so,[24]   30
Would have informed for preparation.[25]

26 *So please you* – "Excuse me (for contradicting you)".

27 *One of my fellows* – "a fellow-servant", another messenger.

28 *had the speed of him* – "came more quickly than he did".

29 *Who* – "and he", the messenger.

30 *scarcely more . . . his message* – "scarcely more (breath) than he used in giving his message".

31 *Give him tending* – "Go and look after him".

32 The messenger leaves, and Lady Macbeth is alone again, her plans one stage further forward. Between now and the arrival of Macbeth she prays for evil power and strength to carry out her purpose.

33 *The raven himself is hoarse.* It was thought that a raven croaking on a house meant that death was near. Here the air is so full of death that the raven is hoarse with croaking.

34 *tend on mortal thoughts; mortal* – "deadly"; "wait on thoughts of murder".

35 *unsex me* – "take away my womanhood". Lady Macbeth takes womanhood as an image of tenderness (as at I.vii.54).

36 *the crown to the toe* – "completely full", from head to foot.

37 *compunctious visitings of nature* – "feelings of kindness (*nature*) which will prick the conscience".

38 *Shake my fell purpose* – ". . . endanger (*Shake*) my savage (*fell*) plans".

39 *keep peace . . . and it* – "prevent the result (*Th' effect*, the murder) and it (the *fell purpose*) from coming together." Lady Macbeth prays that they may not be kept apart, that the result may follow from the purpose.

40 *take my milk for gall* – "take away my milk, and give me gall instead". Milk stands for tenderness, and gall for bitterness.

41 *murdering ministers* – "spirits who attend on murders".

42 *sightless* – "invisible".

43 *wait on* – "attend" (see note 41 above).

44 *pall thee* – "wrap yourself".

45 *the dunnest smoke* – "the darkest smoke", such as rises from the fires of hell.

46 *the blanket of the dark.* The blanket is for night, whose darkness will cover up the murder of Duncan. Lady Macbeth prays that no good spirit in heaven shall bring light into this darkness and reveal the evil.

47 *Hold, hold!* – "Keep back (your hand); stop!".

48 Lady Macbeth's prayer rises to a height of dramatic power as Macbeth comes; she thinks first of the promise of the weird sisters that her husband shall be king, and then they speak of Duncan.

49 *by the all-hail* – "according to the greeting (of the weird sisters)".

50 *transported* – "delighted", and also "carried away".

51 *I feel now . . . instant* – "I now feel the future in the present". She is carried away with delight, and what has been promised has become real and actual to her.

MESSENGER

So please you,[26] it is true: our thane is coming;
One of my fellows[27] had the speed of him,[28]
Who,[29] almost dead for breath, had scarcely more
Than would make up his message.[30]

LADY MACBETH

                        Give him tending:[31]   35
He brings great news. [*Exit* Messenger][32] The raven
  himself is hoarse[33]
That croaks the fatal entrance of Duncan
Under my battlements. Come, you spirits
That tend on mortal thoughts,[34] unsex me[35] here,
And fill me, from the crown to the toe,[36] top-full   40
Of direst cruelty! make thick my blood,
Stop up th' access and passage to remorse;
That no compunctious visitings of nature[37]
Shake my fell purpose,[38] nor keep peace between
Th' effect and it![39] Come to my woman's breasts,   45
And take my milk for gall,[40] you murdering ministers,[41]
Wherever in your sightless[42] substances
You wait on[43] nature's mischief! Come, thick night,
And pall thee[44] in the dunnest smoke[45] of hell,
That my keen knife see not the wound it makes,   50
Nor heaven peep through the blanket of the dark[46]
To cry, "Hold, hold!"[47]

Enter MACBETH[48]

                Great Glamis! worthy Cawdor!
Greater than both, by the all-hail,[49] hereafter!
Thy letters have transported[50] me beyond
This ignorant present, and I feel now   55
The future in the instant.[51]

52 *as he purposes* – "according to his plans".

53 *Your face . . . strange matters.* Lady Macbeth fears that the look on her husband's face will make people wonder, for she can "read" his fear there; she therefore begins to show him how to add to his strength of purpose.

54 *To beguile . . . the time* – "If you want to deceive (*beguile*) the world (*the time*, the (present) world), look like the world"; act in the normal way, and no one will notice you. The idea is given an image in the flower and the serpent (lines 63–4 below).

55 *provided for.* Macbeth has come to see that Duncan is provided with lodging for the night; but now provision will be made for his murder.

56 *into my despatch* – "under my direction".

57 *Which shall to all . . . masterdom* – "(And this business) shall give us alone (*solely*) the power (*sway*) and mastery of kingship for all the rest of our lives".

58 *Only look up clear.* Macbeth's face must not give him away; he must keep his looks "clear" of evil signs.

59 *To alter favour . . . fear* – "It is always a sign of fear when the look on one's face (*favour*) changes".

The temple-haunting martlet[4] (Scene VI)

MACBETH

My dearest love,
Duncan comes here tonight.

LADY MACBETH

And when goes hence?

MACBETH

Tomorrow, as he purposes.[52]

LADY MACBETH

O! never
Shall sun that morrow see!
Your face, my thane, is as a book, where men   60
May read strange matters.[53] To beguile the time,
Look like the time,[54] bear welcome in your eye,
Your hand, your tongue: look like the innocent flower
But be the serpent under 't. He that 's coming
Must be provided for;[55] and you shall put   65
This night's great business into my despatch;[56]
Which shall to all our nights and days to come
Give solely sovereign sway and masterdom.[57]

MACBETH

We will speak further.

LADY MACBETH

Only look up clear;[58]
To alter favour ever is to fear.[59]   70
Leave all the rest to me.

[Exeunt

37

(I.vi) Duncan, with his sons, his lords, and his attendants, arrives in front of Macbeth's castle. The king and Banquo agree that it is pleasantly situated and has a pleasing air of peace about it. Lady Macbeth comes out to greet them with fulsome professions of service.

1 *The same*, i.e. the same place as the last scene, Inverness. The king, his sons and his lords are shown in front of the castle. Inside the castle, Macbeth and his wife prepare for murder; outside, to point the contrast, Duncan and Banquo find the situation of the castle pleasant and sweet, a home of peace, as they think.

2 *seat* – "position".

3 *the air* (line 1) . . . *our gentle senses* – "The air makes itself agreeable (*recommends itself*) to my gentle senses in its freshness and sweetness".

4 *This guest . . . martlet*. Banquo is undoubtedly pointing out the house-martin, a bird which settles in Britain for the summer months (*This guest of summer*), and flies south in the autumn. This bird builds its nest of mud and straw, and sets it against the outside walls of houses. (Banquo refers to this nest when he speaks of the *pendent bed, and procreant cradle* in line 8.) It is said to be *temple-haunting*, "frequenting churches", for martins and swallows often fly about inside country churches (see illustration p. 36).

5 *approve* – "prove".

6 *his loved mansionry* – "the building for a house which he loves (to live in)", i.e. the nest.

7 *the heaven's breath* – "the wind".

8 *wooingly* – "delightfully"; to *woo* is to delight or attract, and is especially used of lovers.

9 *jutty* – a part of a building which stands out (juts out) from the rest.

10 *coign of vantage* – a corner (*coign*) of a building giving a good view.

11 *but* – "except" – connects with *no* in the line before: "(there is) no jutty, frieze . . . except (those on which) this bird has made . . ."; i.e. "there is no jutty, frieze . . . on which this bird has not made . . ."

12 *pendent*; the nest seems to hang from the outer walls.

13 Lady Macbeth greets her guests with fulsome compliments; but the gentle pleasures described by the king and Banquo are, to the audience, a complete contradiction of the true air of her evil thoughts. Duncan sees her as she enters, calls attention to her (*See, see!* . . .), and then begins to speak to her.

14 *The love that follows us* (line 11) . . . *for your trouble*. – "The love (shown by hosts) which waits upon me is sometimes disagreeable to me; yet I thank (the host for it, recognising it) as love. From this you will learn to ask God to reward me (*yield us*) for your trouble, and thank me for it".

15 *point* – "detail".

16 *Were* – "would be".

17 *single* – "weak".

18 *contend Against* – "set up against, compare".

19 *wherewith* – "with which".

20 *our house* – not just the building but the family living in it.

21 *those of old*, i.e. those honours which we have held for a long time.

Scene VI. The same.[1] Before the castle.
Hautboys and torches. Enter DUNCAN, MALCOLM,
DONALBAIN, BANQUO, LENOX, MACDUFF,
ROSSE, ANGUS, *and* Attendants.

DUNCAN

This castle hath a pleasant seat:[2] the air
Nimbly and sweetly recommends itself
Unto our gentle senses.[3]

*dramatic
irony*

BANQUO

This guest of summer,
The temple-haunting martlet,[4] does approve,[5]
By his loved mansionry,[6] that the heaven's breath[7]   5
Smells wooingly[8] here: no jutty,[9] frieze,
Buttress, nor coign of vantage,[10] but[11] this bird
Hath made his pendent[12] bed, and procreant cradle:
Where they most breed and haunt, I have observed,
The air is delicate.

Enter LADY MACBETH[13]

DUNCAN

See, see! our honoured hostess. —   10
[*To* LADY MACBETH] The love that follows us sometime is
  our trouble,
Which still we thank as love. Herein I teach you,
How you shall bid God yield us for your pains,
And thank us for your trouble.[14]

LADY MACBETH

All our service,
In every point[15] twice done, and then done double,   15
Were[16] poor and single[17] business to contend
Against[18] those honours deep and broad, wherewith[19]
Your majesty loads our house:[20] for those of old,[21]

39

22 *late* – "recent".

23 *heaped up to them*, suggesting a great pile of honour given them, continues the image with *loads* in the previous line.

24 *We rest your hermits* – "we remain nothing but people who can pray for you (*your hermits*)", for we cannot pay you·in any other way.

25 *We coursed him at the heels* – "I followed him from close behind". *To course* is to follow animals in hunting, but in fact it is Macbeth and his wife who are hunting down Duncan; the king's little joke is painfully ironical to the audience.

26 *had a purpose To be his purveyor;* a *purveyor* was an officer who travelled before the king during his journeys, preparing food and lodging for the royal party. The king says, "(I) had an idea that I might be *his* purveyor" (and not he mine, which would be the arrangement expected). It is another of Duncan's little jokes, charged with irony in the dramatic situation.

27 *his great love, sharp as his spur . . .* Again the king uses words which mean more to the audience than they do to him. He here compares Macbeth's love to a spur which is sharp, like an instrument of death.

28 *hath holp him To his home* – ". . . has helped (*holp*) him to arrive home".

29 *Your servants ever* (line 25) *. . . to return your own.* "Your servants always keep their servants (*theirs*), themselves, and their property (*what ·is theirs*) accountable (*in compt*) to you; (they are ready) to give an account of it (*make their audit*) when you wish (*at your highness' pleasure*) and always to return to you what is yours." Lady Macbeth expresses in very formal style the idea that as the king is master of everything in the land he has a right to anything they can do for him or give him.

30 *graces* – "favours".

31 *By your leave* – "with your permission". Duncan asks politely to be taken to Macbeth.

(I.vii) The welcoming meal for Duncan and his lords is in progress. Macbeth leaves the banqueting hall and stands aside to think of the deed he is about to do; he is frightened of what it might lead to. His wife comes from the hall to look for him, and she succeeds in convincing him that the murder can be carried out.

1 *sewer* – "chief waiter".

2 *divers* – "various".

3 *If it were done . . . done quickly* – "If it (the murder) were completely finished when we do it, then it would be a good thing if it were done quickly".

4 *If the assassination . . . his surcease success* – ". . . if the actual murder could catch up (*trammel up*) the consequences, and could come to a final result (*success*) with Duncan's death (*surcease*) (then again it would be a good thing to do it quickly)".

5 *that but this blow* – "if only this blow".

6 *the be-all and the end-all* – "the existence and conclusion in itself". The point is, again, that the murderous blow is *not* a thing existing alone and complete in itself, but leads to other things.

40

And the late[22] dignities heaped up to them,[23]
We rest your hermits.[24]

DUNCAN

                    Where 's the Thane of Cawdor?   20
We coursed him at the heels,[25] and had a purpose
To be his purveyor:[26] but he rides well;
And his great love, sharp as his spur,[27] hath holp him
To his home[28] before us. Fair and noble hostess,
We are your guest tonight.

LADY MACBETH

                    Your servants ever   25
Have theirs, themselves, and what is theirs, in compt,
To make their audit at your highness' pleasure,
Still to return your own.[29]

DUNCAN

                    Give me your hand;
Conduct me to mine host: we love him highly,
And shall continue our graces[30] towards him.   30
By your leave,[31] hostess.

                                        [*Exeunt*

Scene VII. The same. A room in the castle.
Hautboys and torches. Enter, and pass over the stage,
a Sewer,[1] *and divers*[2] Servants *with dishes and service.*
Then enter MACBETH.

MACBETH

[*Aside*] If it were done when 't is done, then 't were well
It were done quickly:[3] if the assassination
Could trammel up the consequence, and catch
With his surcease success;[4] that but this blow[5]
Might be the be-all and the end-all[6] here,   5

41

7 *But here* – "even here (i.e. in this world) only".

8 *this bank and shoal of time; shoal* – "a narrow strip of land between water". The image is of life as a narrow bank thrusting into the great seas of eternity (see illustration p. 44).

9 *jump* – "risk".

10 *the life to come* – "the life in the next world, after death", and what might happen there.

11 *in these cases* – "in situations such as these".

12 *still* – "regularly".

13 *that* – "in that".

14 *we but teach* (line 8) . . . *plague th' inventor* – "We only (*but*) teach others how to murder (*Bloody instructions*), and the directions, when they are understood, come back to trouble the person who thought of them (*th' inventor*)".

15 *this even-handed justice . . . our own lips; justice* is figured with hands holding equal weights, and therefore completely fair, one side affecting the other. Justice, always fair, offers (*commends*) to us the poisoned contents of the cup (*chalice*) which we have prepared for someone else.

16 *He's* – "The king is".

17 *in double trust* – "entrusted (to me) in two ways". Macbeth is Duncan's relative and his subject, and also his host, as he goes on to say.

18 *Strong both . . . deed* – "both of which (i.e. being a relative and a subject) being strong (arguments) against the deed (or murder)".

19 *faculties* – "(kingly) powers".

20 *meek* – "meekly".

21 *clear* – "free from fault".

22 *office* – "duty, work" (of being king).

23 *trumpet-tongued* – "with tongues as loud as trumpets", and sounding out, like trumpets, to all the world.

24 *taking-off* – "murder".

25 *Pity* for Duncan will blow like the wind into every eye (line 24) when the murder is done, and none will be free from tears. This pity seems weak against Macbeth's evil plans, but it may be his downfall. It is compared to a helpless child who is nevertheless riding on the great wind (*Striding the blast*, line 22), and to the angelic children of heaven (*heaven's cherubin*, line 22) who can, although children, ride the wild horses of the sky (*horsed Upon the sightless couriers of the air*, lines 22–3). Both are examples of weak pity controlling fierce strength.

26 *cherubin* – "cherubs, angelic children".

27 *horsed* – "riding on horseback".

28 *sightless* – "invisible" (compare I.v.47 and the note to it).

29 *couriers* – "fast horses", i.e. the winds.

30 *That* – "so that".

31 *tears shall drown the wind.* When wind blows into the eyes, they "water", become wet with tears. When the wind of pity for Duncan blows, every eye shall be so full of tears that the wind itself will be "drowned".

32 *I have no spur* (line 25) . . . *on the other* – "I have nothing to push forward my desire (*no spur To prick the sides of my intent;* he speaks as if it were a horse and he a rider), except hopeful (*Vaulting*) ambition, which is like a rider who, in jumping on to his horse, misses the saddle (*o'erleaps itself*) and falls off on the other . . ." – he is about to say "side", but Lady Macbeth enters and interrupts him. He has the ambition but lacks the strength of purpose which would be the effective spur to action (see illustration p. 46).

33 We have heard how Macbeth's strength fails him as he thinks of the deed and its consequences. Now Lady Macbeth enters, and persuades him that the murder should be carried through.

continued on page 44

But here[7] upon this bank and shoal of time,[8]
We 'd jump[9] the life to come.[10] – But, in these cases,[11]
We still[12] have judgement here, that[13] we but teach
Bloody instructions, which, being taught, return
To plague th' inventor:[14] this even-handed justice   10
Commends th' ingredients of our poisoned chalice
To our own lips.[15] He 's[16] here in double trust:[17]
First, as I am his kinsman and his subject,
Strong both against the deed;[18] then, as his host,
Who should against his murderer shut the door,   15
Not bear the knife myself. Besides, this Duncan
Hath borne his faculties[19] so meek[20] hath been
So clear[21] in his great office,[22] that his virtues
Will plead like angels, trumpet-tongued,[23] against
The deep damnation of his taking-off;[24]   20
And pity,[25] like a naked new-born babe,
Striding the blast, or heaven's cherubin,[26] horsed[27]
Upon the sightless[28] couriers[29] of the air,
Shall blow the horrid deed in every eye,
That[30] tears shall drown the wind.[31] – I have no spur   25
To prick the sides of my intent, but only
Vaulting ambition, which o'erleaps itself
And falls on the other –[32]

Enter LADY MACBETH[33]

How now! what news?

LADY MACBETH

He has almost supped.[34] Why have you left the chamber?[35]

MACBETH

Hath he asked for me?

43

34 *almost supped* – "almost finished supper".

35 *the chamber*, i.e. the room where they have been eating. Macbeth does not answer this question, but hurries on to another.

36 *of late* – "recently".

37 *bought* – "acquired".

38 *Golden opinions* – "a shining (i.e. honourable) reputation".

39 *Which would . . . newest gloss* – "which should be worn now, while they are still new and shining". He speaks of the reputation as if it were clothing for the body.

40 *Was the hope . . . dressed yourself?* Lady Macbeth takes up the image of reputation as clothing: "Was the ambition (as opposed to the reputation) in which you once dressed yourself drunk (i.e. false)?"

41 *green* – "sickly", a colour of weakness and fear, as shown in the face.

42 *Such I account thy love* – "I consider your love to be of the same sort (i.e. green and pale)".

43 *afeard* – "frightened".

44 *the same in thine . . . in desire* – "the same person in action and bravery as in desire"; is he frightened to be the person he wishes to be and to do the thing he wishes to do?

45 *Wouldst thou have . . .* – "Do you want to have . . ."

46 *the ornament of life* is the crown, referred to here as the crowning success of Macbeth's ambition.

47 *wait upon* – "attend", and so "go along with".

48 The *poor cat i' the adage* wanted to catch some fish, but would not wet her paws to do so.

49 *peace* – "be quiet".

50 *I dare do . . . a man* – "I dare do everything that it is fitting for a man to do".

51 *Who dares . . . is none* – "(The man) who dares do more (than that) is no man at all".

52 *What beast was 't . . . enterprise to me?* – "(If it was not a man) what beast was it that made you tell me of these plans (*break this enterprise*)?"

Lady Macbeth now drops the familiar *thou* used for relatives, and begins to address her husband formally as *you*.

53 *When you durst do it* – "When you *did* dare to do it".

54 *Nor time nor place . . . make both* – "Then neither the time nor the place had come together (*Did . . . adhere*) (as suitable for the murder of the king), and yet you wanted to arrange both (i.e. the time and the place)".

this bank and shoal[8]

44

Having 2nd thoughts

LADY MACBETH

Know you not he has?   30

MACBETH   *He won't do it*

We will proceed no further in this business;
He hath honoured me of late;[36] and I have bought[37]
Golden opinions[38] from all sorts of people,
Which would be worn now in their newest gloss,[39]
Not cast aside so soon.

wearing

wearing
Kasophron.

LADY MACBETH

Was the hope drunk,
Wherein you dressed yourself?[40] hath it slept since,   35
And wakes it now, to look so green[41] and pale
At what it did so freely? From this time
Such I account thy love.[42] Art thou afeard[43]
To be the same in thine own act and valour,   40
As thou art in desire?[44] Wouldst thou have[45] that
Which thou esteem'st the ornament of life,[46]
And live a coward in thine own esteem,
Letting "I dare not" wait upon[47] "I would,"
Like the poor cat i' the adage?[48]

she knows that he wants it but makes him out a coward

MACBETH

Pr'ythee, peace.[49]   45
I dare do all that may become a man;[50]
Who dares do more is none.[51]

*He speaks the truth. She
plays more manly to
act like a question
everyone a man. But become*

LADY MACBETH

What beast was 't then
That made you break this enterprise to me?[52]
When you durst do it,[53] then you were a man;
And, to be more than what you were, you would   50
Be so much more the man. Nor time nor place
Did then adhere, and yet you would make both:[54]

*man ≠ woman
≠ beast*

55 *They,* i.e. the time and the place.

56 *that* refers to *their fitness;* "that which is their fitness".

57 *Does unmake you* – "ruins you, ruins your self-confidence".

58 *had I so sworn . . . done to this* – "if I had sworn as strongly (to do that, i.e. kill the baby) as you have done to do this (i.e. murder the king)".

59 *We fail!* – ". . . then we fail (and there is nothing more we can do about it)". But some think she is questioning what Macbeth has just said: *We fail?* ("Of course we shan't fail; why have you doubts about it?") If this is the right explanation, *But* in the next line means "only".

60 *screw your . . . sticking-place.* The image here is of a stringed musical instrument; it has pegs in the handle which are turned until the strings fixed to them are stretched tight. Then each peg is pressed in to make the string firm. Macbeth must tighten his courage (*screw* it) until it is firmly fixed (at the *sticking-place;* see illustration p. 48).

61 (*Whereto the rather . . . invite him*) – "his day's hard journey will very likely persuade him to do this (i.e. sleep) soundly". The comparative *rather* suggests that he is more likely to sleep soundly on this night than on normal nights.

62 *wassail* – "merry-making".

63 *convince* – "overpower".

64 Memory is *the warder of the brain,* as the chamberlains are warders of the king. By overpowering one she will overpower the other.

65 (*memory . . .*) *Shall be a fume . . . limbeck only* – ". . . memory, which guards the brain, shall (with drunkenness) become a foul gas, and the brain itself nothing but an alembic"; *fume* – "gas", especially a kind of gas which was supposed to rise from the stomach to the head when too much wine was drunk; *receipt* – "receptacle, the thing which receives or holds", so *the receipt of reason* is the brain; *limbeck* – "alembic", a vessel once used for getting and collecting pure liquid from gas (see *alembic* in the glossary; see illustration p. 49).

66 *natures* – "beings".

67 *What not put upon* – "What can we not blame (his officers) for?"

68 *spongy* – "drunken", since they had filled themselves with drink like sponges.

69 *quell* – "murder".

70 *Bring forth* – "Bear" (as a mother).

71 *thy undaunted mettle* – "the fearless material of which you are made"; *mettle* – "strong material", and so "courage".

72 *received* – "accepted as the truth".

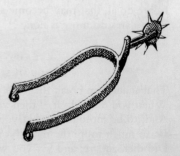

Spur[32]

46

They[55] have made themselves, and that[56] their fitness now
Does unmake you.[57] I have given suck, and know
How tender 't is to love the babe that milks me: 55
I would, while it was smiling in my face,
Have plucked my nipple from his boneless gums,
And dashed the brains out, had I so sworn as you
Have done to this.[58]

MACBETH

If we should fail, –   *= practicality
no morality
any more*

LADY MACBETH

We fail![59]

But screw your courage to the sticking-place[60]   60
And we 'll not fail. When Duncan is asleep
(Whereto the rather shall his day's hard journey
Soundly invite him),[61] his two chamberlains
Will I with wine and wassail[62] so convince,[63]
That memory, the warder of the brain,[64]   65
Shall be a fume, and the receipt of reason
A limbeck only:[65] when in swinish sleep
Their drenchèd natures[66] lie, as in a death,
What cannot you and I perform upon
Th' unguarded Duncan? What not put upon[67]   70
His spongy[68] officers, who shall bear the guilt
Of our great quell?[69]

MACBETH

Bring forth[70] men-children only!
For thy undaunted mettle[71] should compose
Nothing but males. Will it not be received,[72]
When we have marked with blood those sleepy two   75
Of his own chamber, and used their very daggers,
That they have done 't?

47

73 *Who dares receive it other* – "Who will dare to accept it otherwise (than as the truth)?"

74 *As* – "since".

75 *our griefs and clamour* – "our loud cries of sorrow".

76 *Upon* – "at".

77 *settled* – "decided".

78 *bend up Each corporal agent* – "make ready each faculty of my body".

79 *Away* – "Let us go away!"

80 *mock the time . . . show* – "deceive the world (*the time*) with a happy face (*fairest show*)".

screw your courage to the sticking-place[60]

LADY MACBETH

Who dares receive it other,[73]
As[74] we shall make our griefs and clamour[75] roar
Upon[76] his death?

MACBETH

I am settled,[77] and bend up   80
Each corporal agent[78] to this terrible feat.
[Away,[79] and mock the time with fairest show:[80]]
False face must hide what the false heart doth know.

[*Exeunt*

evil   [*v/w*]
morally damaged

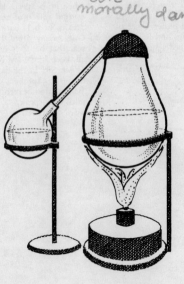

A limbeck[65]

(II.i) It is now far into the night, yet Banquo, who has attended the king to bed, is still in the courtyard with his son. Uneasy thoughts, he says, make him disinclined to sleep. He is surprised that Macbeth, attended by a servant with a torch, is not yet in bed either. They speak for a moment about the recent prophecies, and Banquo and Fleance leave. Macbeth sends a servant to ask Lady Macbeth to ring the bell when his drink is ready. This is an agreed sign that the time is right for the murder. Left alone, Macbeth sees the vision of a dagger placed ready for him to clutch. Drops of blood appear on it; he thinks of wicked deeds done under cover of night. The bell rings and he walks towards Duncan's bedchamber.

1 *How goes the night* – "What time of night is it?"

2 *is down* – "has set".

3 *she*, the moon.

4 *I take 't* – "I assume (from what you have just said)".

5 *husbandry in heaven* – "the sky is being economical (by blowing all its candles out)"; i.e. the stars are not shining.

6 *Take thee that, too* – "Take that as well"; *that* is something other than the sword which Banquo has just handed to his son; perhaps it is an outer coat.

7 *A heavy summons* – "A solemn call (to do something)".

8 *would not* – "do not wish to".

9 *the cursèd thoughts* are dreams which his heavy spirits cause him to see when he is asleep. He prays to the *merciful powers* of heaven that these dreams be held back.

10 *Give me my sword.* His fears are so real that he feels he should, after all, keep his sword by him.

11 *What, Sir!* In the darkness, lit only by two torches, Macbeth and Banquo do not recognise each other until they speak.

12 *a-bed* – "in bed".

ACT TWO

Scene I. The same. A court within the castle.
Enter BANQUO, *and* FLEANCE *with a torch before him.*

BANQUO

How goes the night,[1] boy?

FLEANCE

The moon is down;[2] I have not heard the clock.

BANQUO

And she[3] goes down at twelve.

FLEANCE

                I take 't,[4] 't is later, Sir

BANQUO

Hold, take my sword. – There 's husbandry in heaven;[5]
Their candles are all out. – Take thee that, too.[6]   5
A heavy summons[7] lies like lead upon me,
And yet I would not[8] sleep: merciful powers!
Restrain in me the cursèd thoughts[9] that nature
Gives way to in repose! – Give me my sword.[10]

Enter MACBETH, *and a* Servant *with a torch.*

[*To* MACBETH] Who 's there?   10

MACBETH

A friend.

BANQUO

What, Sir![11] not yet at rest? The king 's a-bed:[12]
He hath been in unusual pleasure, and

51

13 *largess* – "generous gifts".

14 *offices* – "the part of a house used by servants".

15 *This diamond . . . kind hostess* – "He greets your wife with this diamond, calling her (*By the name of*) a most kind hostess".

16 *shut up . . . content* – "(The king) has finished (*shut up*) (the evening's entertainment) in boundless pleasure".

17 *Being unprepared* (line 17) *. . . free have wrought* – "Because we were not prepared (for the royal visit), our wishes, which would otherwise (*else*) have been effected more generously (*should free have wrought*), led only to inefficient service (*became the servant to defect*)"; *defect* ("inefficiency") was the master, and "our wishes" the servants, and therefore less powerful.

18 *when we can entreat . . . that business* – "When I might beg a free hour (*an hour to serve*) (with you), I would like to pass it in talking about that business".

19 *At your kind'st leisure* – "When you are free, and so kind (as to do what you suggest)."

20 *If you shall . . . 't is* – "If you will keep on my side, with my party (*cleave to my consent*) when it is formed . . ." But perhaps *when 't is* refers to the talk, not the party:
"If you will take my part, when we have it (i.e. the talk I have just suggested) . . ."

21 *So I lose none* (line 26) *. . . be counselled* – "So long as (*So*) I lose none (i.e. no honour) in trying to make it greater, but always (*still*) keep my heart (*bosom*) free (from sin) (*franchised*) and my faithfulness clear (i.e. to one man only, the king), I shall listen to your advice".

Is this a dagger which I see before me?

Sent forth great largess[13] to your offices.[14]
This diamond he greets your wife withal,   15
By the name of most kind hostess,[15] and shut up
In measureless content.[16]

MACBETH

       Being unprepared,
Our will became the servant to defect,
Which else should free have wrought.[17]

BANQUO

              All 's well.
I dreamt last night of the three weird sisters: 20
To you they have showed some truth.

MACBETH

           I think not of them:
Yet, when we can entreat an hour to serve,
We would spend it in some words upon that business,[18]
If you would grant the time.

BANQUO

         At your kind'st leisure.[19]

MACBETH

If you shall cleave to my consent, when 't is,[20]   25
It shall make honour for you.

BANQUO

         So I lose none
In seeking to augment it, but still keep
My bosom franchised, and allegiance clear,
I shall be counselled.[21]

22 *the while* – "for the time being, until we meet again".

23 *the like* – "the same (good wishes)".

24 *bid thy mistress . . . upon the bell* – "tell your mistress to ring the bell when my drink is ready". This is clearly a signal which Macbeth and his wife have already arranged together.

25 *I have thee . . . still* – "I cannot hold you, yet I see you all the time". It is only a vision.

26 *sensible To feeling as to sight* – "perceptible (*sensible*, what may be perceived by the senses) by touch as well as by sight".

27 *creation* – "what is created".

28 *this*, i.e. a real dagger, his own.

29 *Thou marshall'st me the way* – "You guide me along the way", to the room where Duncan is sleeping.

30 *such an instrument* – "an instrument of this sort", i.e. the dagger.

31 *Mine eyes are made . . . all the rest* – "My eyes are either deceived by (*made the fools o'*) the other senses, or more trustworthy than all of them." He must believe either that his eyes tell him the truth (that there is a dagger in front of him, because he can see it), or that his other senses are to be trusted (that there is no dagger, because he cannot feel it).

32 *dudgeon* – "hilt".

33 *gouts* – "drops".

34 *Which was not so before* – "and it was not like this before". The drops of blood have just appeared.

35 *informs Thus* – "forms, takes this shape".

36 *Now o'er the one half world*, i.e. over that "half world" or hemisphere where it is night.

37 *wicked dreams . . . sleep* – "wicked dreams deceive (*abuse*) the privacy of sleep".

Sleep is said to be *curtained* because beds used to stand in large rooms with curtains drawn round them for privacy. But night itself, Macbeth hopes, shall be a curtain covering his crime (see illustration p. 58).

38 *Hecate's offerings*, i.e. offerings in ceremonies to Hecate, the goddess of witchcraft.

39 *Murder* is personified.

40 *Alarumed* is an older form of *alarmed*.

41 *Whose howl's his watch*, i.e. the wolf's howl is the murderer's "watch"; like a watchman, it tells him how the night is passing.

42 *With Tarquin's ravishing strides* – "with swift, silent steps such as Tarquin made . . .". The story of Tarquin, going secretly in the night to ravish the beautiful Lucrece, his hostess and the wife of his friend, comes from Roman history. It is also the subject of Shakespeare's poem *The Rape of Lucrece*.

43 *his design* – "what he plans to do".

44 *Moves like a ghost* completes the sentence whose subject is *withered Murder* (line 52): "withered murder . . . moves like a ghost towards his design".

45 *sure* – "safe".

MACBETH

Good repose the while!²²

BANQUO

Thanks, Sir: the like²³ to you.   30

[*Exeunt* BANQUO *and* FLEANCE

MACBETH

[*To the* Servant] Go, bid thy mistress, when my drink is ready,
She strike upon the bell.²⁴ Get thee to bed. –

brows

[*Exit* Servant

Is this a dagger which I see before me,
The handle toward my hand? [*He speaks to the dagger*] Come,
  let me clutch thee: –
I have thee not, and yet I see thee still.²⁵   35
Art thou not, fatal vision, sensible
To feeling as to sight?²⁶ or art thou but
A dagger of the mind, a false creation,²⁷
Proceeding from the heat-oppressèd brain?
I see thee yet, in form as palpable   40
As this²⁸ which now I draw.
Thou marshall'st me the way²⁹ that I was going;
And such an instrument³⁰ I was to use. –
Mine eyes are made the fools o' the other senses,
Or else worth all the rest:³¹ I see thee still;   45
And on thy blade and dudgeon³² gouts³³ of blood,
Which was not so before.³⁴ – There 's no such thing.
It is the bloody business which informs
Thus³⁵ to mine eyes. – Now o'er the one half world³⁶
Nature seems dead, and wicked dreams abuse   50
The curtained sleep:³⁷ witchcraft celebrates
Pale Hecate's offerings;³⁸ and withered Murder,³⁹
Alarumed⁴⁰ by his sentinel, the wolf,
Whose howl 's his watch,⁴¹ thus with his stealthy pace,
With Tarquin's ravishing strides,⁴² towards his design⁴³   55
Moves like a ghost.⁴⁴ – Thou sure⁴⁵ and firm-set earth,

← unreality can
be deeper than
reality

46 *my where-about* – "the place where I am".

47 *And take the present . . . suits with it* – "And (for fear that the stones) separate the horror of the moment (the murder) from the general situation (*the time*), which is now suitable for it (*suits with it*)".

48 *I threat* for *I threaten*.

49 *Words to the . . . breath gives* – "Words (alone) give breath which is too cold for the heat of deeds"; deeds are "hot", mere talking about them is "cold".

(II.ii) We are to imagine Macbeth actually murdering the king as Lady Macbeth enters; she has drugged the drinks of the two attendants who are at their posts outside the king's bedchamber. Macbeth gives a cry from the king's room which makes his wife fear that he has failed to murder the king and will cause a general alarm. But he comes in and tells her that the deed is done. His hands are covered in blood and he has forgotten to leave the daggers by the attendants so that the crime should appear to be theirs. She takes them back for him, and immediately someone begins knocking at the castle gate. Macbeth is again filled with terror, but his wife, returning from the king's chamber, tells him to wash quickly and put on his night-clothes so that it will look as if he has been asleep.

1 *The same;* a little time has passed, for Macbeth is actually murdering Duncan as Lady Macbeth enters.

2 *That which hath . . . me bold* – "(The wine) which has made (the chamberlains) drunk has given me courage".

3 *Hark! – Peace!* – "Listen! – (No, it is all) quiet!" She thinks she hears some noise from the people in the castle.

4 *the fatal bellman . . . stern'st goodnight.* She compares the call of the owl in the night to the ringing of a bell; the owl, crying out before death, is like the *fatal bellman* who rings a bell before a dead body on its way to burial (*fatal* – "associated with death"). And the *stern'st goodnight* is "the last goodbye", the goodbye of death.

5 *He is about it* – "He (Macbeth) is doing it (now)".

6 *the surfeited grooms . . . with snores* – "The servants, overfull (of drink), mock their responsibility by snoring".

7 *possets* – "hot drinks".

8 *That death . . . live or die* – ". . . so that death and life (*nature*) argue over them (the grooms), as to whether they are alive or dead".

9 [*Within*], i.e. in the inner room.

10 *Alack!* expresses sorrow.

11 *they*, the chamberlains.

Hear not my steps, which way they walk, for fear
Thy very stones prate of my where-about,[46]
And take the present horror from the time,
Which now suits with it.[47] Whiles I threat,[48] he lives: 60
Words to the heat of deeds too cold breath gives.[49]

[*A bell rings*

I go, and it is done: the bell invites me.
Hear it not, Duncan; for it is a knell
That summons thee to heaven or to hell.

[*Exit*

Scene II. The same.[1]
Enter LADY MACBETH.

LADY MACBETH

That which hath made them drunk hath made me bold.[2]
What hath quenched them hath given me fire. – Hark! –
  Peace![3]
It was the owl that shrieked, the fatal bellman,
Which gives the stern'st good-night.[4] He is about it.[5]
The doors are open, and the surfeited grooms
Do mock their charge with snores.[6] I have drugged
  their possets,[7]
That death and nature do contend about them,
Whether they live or die.[8]

MACBETH

[*Within*][9]   Who 's there? – what, ho!

LADY MACBETH

Alack![10] I am afraid they[11] have awaked,
And 't is not done: – the attempt, and not the deed, 10

57

12 *Confounds us* – "brings us to ruin".
13 *their*, the chamberlains'. It was planned to use their daggers for the murder so that the blame should be put on them.
14 *He*, Macbeth.
15 *he*, Duncan.

16 *I had done 't* – "I would have done it (myself)".
17 *the second chamber* – "the second bedroom", the bedroom next to the king's own.
18 *sorry* – "sad". His hands are covered with the blood of Duncan.

The curtained sleep[37] (Scene 1)

Confounds us.[12] – Hark! – I laid their[13] daggers ready;
He[14] could not miss them. – Had he[15] not resembled
My father as he slept, I had done 't.[16] – My husband!

Enter MACBETH

MACBETH

I have done the deed. – Didst thou not hear a noise?

LADY MACBETH

I heard the owl scream, and the crickets cry.   15
Did not you speak?

MACBETH

　　　　When?

LADY MACBETH

　　　　Now.

MACBETH

　　　　　　As I descended?

LADY MACBETH

Ay.

MACBETH

Hark!
Who lies i' the second chamber?[17]

LADY MACBETH

　　　　　Donalbain.

MACBETH

[*Looking at his hands*] This is a sorry[18] sight.   20

59

19 *There 's one . . . in 's sleep* – "There was one of them (the chamberlains) who laughed in his sleep".

20 *That* – "so that".

21 *addressed them Again* – "prepared themselves once more".

22 *lodged* – "in bed, sleeping".

23 *As* – "as if".

24 *these hangman's hands* – "hands covered with blood", like those of a hangman.

25 *Listening their fear* – "Listening to (the expression of) their fear". He found he could not make the people's reply, *Amen* ("let it be so"), to the prayer usually spoken by the priest.

26 *Consider it not so deeply* – "Do not think so deeply about it".

27 *wherefore* – "for what reason; why".

28 *These deeds must not . . . make us mad* – "We must not think in this way of these things you have done; (if we do) so, it will make us mad".

29 *Methought* – "It seemed".

30 *Sleep no more!* Since Macbeth has murdered Duncan in his sleep, this supernatural voice tells him that he himself will never be able to sleep again, for he has murdered Sleep as well as Duncan.

31 *Sleep, that . . . sleave of care* – "sleep, that straightens out into a pattern (*knits up*) the confused mass (*ravelled sleave*) of care". Care is imagined as a mass of silk unworked into threads, each thread being a problem or worry. Sleep straightens out these threads of worries into a clear pattern, and they are worries no longer.

32 *sore labour's bath* – "a (refreshing) bath after heavy (*sore*) work".

LADY MACBETH

A foolish thought, to say a sorry sight.

MACBETH

There 's one did laugh in 's sleep,[19] and one cried, "Murder!"
That[20] they did wake each other: I stood and heard them;
But they did say their prayers, and addressed them
Again[21] to sleep.

LADY MACBETH

There are two lodged[22] together.   25

MACBETH

One cried, "God bless us!" and, "Amen," the other,
As[23] they had seen me with these hangman's hands.[24]
Listening their fear,[25] I could not say, "Amen,"
When they did say, "God bless us!"

LADY MACBETH

      Consider it not so deeply.[26]

MACBETH

But wherefore[27] could not I pronounce "Amen"?   30
I had most need of blessing, and "Amen"
Stuck in my throat.

LADY MACBETH

    These deeds must not be thought
After these ways: so, it will make us mad.[28]

MACBETH

Methought[29] I heard a voice cry, "Sleep no more![30]
Macbeth does murder sleep," – the innocent sleep;   35
Sleep, that knits up the ravelled sleave of care,[31]
The death of each day's life, sore labour's bath,[32]

33 *great nature's second course.* In Shakespeare's day the second course was the main part of the meal. Waking life is imagined as the first course, which gives some food for existence; but it is sleep which gives the greatest strength for life and is the *chief nourisher* (line 39).

34 *unbend* – "allow to become loose".

35 *brainsickly* – "as with a sick brain".

36 *this filthy witness* is the blood on his hands, a "witness" or sign of the murder.

37 *I'll go no more* – "I'll not go back again (to the king's room)".

38 *Infirm* – "Weak".

39 *a painted devil* was an image of a devil painted in bright colours and used in popular stage performances. Only children are frightened by such things, because they think the devils are alive; as she knows Duncan is not alive, she has nothing to fear from him.

40 *I'll gild the . . . grooms withal* – "I'll paint the faces of the chamberlains with it (the golden blood)". *To gild* is to colour with gold, and blood was sometimes spoken of as golden; see, e.g. II.iii.109.

Balm of hurt minds, great nature's second course,[33]
Chief nourisher in life's feast; –

LADY MACBETH

What do you mean?

MACBETH

Still it cried, "Sleep no more!" to all the house: 40
"Glamis hath murdered sleep, and therefore Cawdor
Shall sleep no more, Macbeth shall sleep no more!"

LADY MACBETH

Who was it that thus cried? Why, worthy thane,
You do unbend[34] your noble strength, to think
So brainsickly[35] of things. Go, get some water,   45
And wash this filthy witness[36] from your hand. –
Why did you bring these daggers from the place?
They must lie there; go, carry them, and smear
The sleepy grooms with blood.

MACBETH

I 'll go no more:[37]
I am afraid to think what I have done;   50
Look on 't again I dare not.

LADY MACBETH

Infirm[38] of purpose!
Give me the daggers. The sleeping and the dead
Are but as pictures; 't is the eye of childhood
That fears a painted devil.[39] If he do bleed,
I 'll gild the faces of the grooms withal,[40]   55
For it must seem their guilt.

[*Exit. Knocking within*

41 *How is 't with me* – "What is the matter with me".

42 *Neptune's.* Neptune is god of the sea.

43 *No, this my hand* (line 60) . . . *one red* – "No, this hand of mine is more likely (than being made clean by all the ocean) to turn red (*incarnadine*) the great gathering of seas (*The multitudinous seas*), making the green (of the water) one (mass of) red".

44 *I shame* – "I should be ashamed".

45 *retire we* – "let us go (to our room)".

46 *How easy is it then!* – "Then it will be easy (to deceive everyone)".

47 *Your constancy . . . unattended* – "Your firmness of mind has deserted you and left you defenceless."

48 *lest occasion . . . to be watchers* – ". . . in case we are called, because of something happening (*occasion*, some happening or other), and we are found to be out of bed (*watchers*, not sleepers)".

49 *Be not lost . . . your thoughts* – "Do not be so weakly (*poorly*) lost in thought".

50 *To know . . . know myself* – "If I must know my deed, then it would be best for me to lose all knowledge of myself".

51 *I would thou couldst!* – "I wish you (i.e. the person knocking) could!"

(II.iii) A porter, still drunk from the party, goes to open the gate as the knocking continues. Eventually he lets in Macduff and Lenox; Macduff had the night before been told by the king to wake him early. Macbeth enters, and after a few words Macduff goes to the king's chamber. He quickly returns, announcing that the king has been murdered. The bell is rung and Lady Macbeth comes in, supposedly awakened by the alarm. The nobles go in to see the king's body, and Malcolm and Donalbain are told of their father's death. Macbeth admits to having killed the king's attendants in his fury, and Lady Macbeth pretends to faint. They agree to dress quickly and meet in the castle hall. But the two princes decide for their own safety to leave the country.

1 *Porter* – "gate-keeper", who, drunk from the party given in honour of the king, makes his way to the gate at the noise of the knocking.

His speech is difficult to explain in some places, for three reasons: he is drunk; he speaks in a loose, conversational style; and he hints at a number of things which were familiar to Shakespeare's audiences but are strange to us. Much can, however, be understood without difficulty if it is remembered that the porter pretends he is in charge of the gates of hell.

2 *old turning the key* – "a lot of key-turning", because so many people are coming to hell.

MACBETH

Whence is that knocking? –
How is 't with me,[41] when every noise appals me?
What hands are here? Ha! they pluck out mine eyes.
Will all great Neptune's[42] ocean wash this blood
Clean from my hand? No, this my hand will rather   60
The multitudinous seas incarnadine,
Making the green one red.[43]

Re-enter LADY MACBETH

LADY MACBETH

My hands are of your colour; but I shame[44]
To wear a heart so white. [*Knock*] I hear a knocking
At the south entry: retire we[45] to our chamber.   65
A little water clears us of this deed:
How easy is it then![46] Your constancy
Hath left you unattended.[47] – [*Knock*] Hark! more knocking.
Get on your night-gown, lest occasion call us,
And show us to be watchers.[48] – Be not lost   70
So poorly in your thoughts.[49]

MACBETH

To know my deed, 't were best not know myself.[50]

                                        [*Knock*
Wake Duncan with thy knocking: I would thou couldst![51]

                                        [*Exeunt*

Scene III. The same.
Enter a Porter.[1]

                                        [*Knocking within*

PORTER

Here 's a knocking indeed! If a man were porter of hell-gate,
he should have old turning the key.[2] [*Knocking*] Knock, knock,

3 *i' the name of Belzebub:* Belzebub, more often spelt Beelzebub, is a name for the devil.

4 *on the expectation of plenty* – "because plenty (of food) was expected"; and plenty of food would bring down the prices which the farmer could expect for his produce. The joke doubtless refers to some particular event which the audience Shakespeare wrote for would remember at once.

5 *come in time* perhaps means "come in, in (good) time".

6 *napkins* – "handkerchiefs", which would be useful to wipe off sweat in the heat of hell.

7 *about you* – "on you', in the pockets or attached to the clothing.

8 *for 't* – "for what you have done".

9 *'Faith* is short for "In faith"; he swears by his faith in God.

10 *an equivocator* is a person who avoids telling the truth by using words with more than one meaning. At about the time *Macbeth* was being written a Jesuit named Henry Garnet "equivocated" while he was on trial by saying one thing and then something opposite to it, although he had promised to speak the truth. A good deal of attention was paid to this trial, and so to equivocators in general.

11 *that could swear . . . either scale.* Justice, like a pair of scales, weighs one point of view against another. The equivocator swore he spoke the truth in both the scales, both for and against the matter.

12 *treason enough for God's sake.* In Shakespeare's day most English people feared that the Roman Catholic church might overthrow the power of the Protestant king, James I. The porter here thinks of a man who betrayed his country "for God's sake", i.e. for his religion.

13 *could not equivocate to heaven.* As he lied, he was not sent to heaven for his playing with words, but to hell.

14 *an English tailor . . . A French hose; French hose* – "trousers made in the French 'way", i.e. showy, made for display (the English thought the French enjoyed wearing clothes like this). The joke here seems to be simply that the tailor was English and the trousers "French". But tailors were, in general, looked upon as being dishonest people.

15 *roast your goose.* A tailor's "goose" is a flat iron for smoothing clothes (it has a handle like a goose's neck). The porter associates *tailor* with *goose*, the bird, and says that the goose belonging to the tailor may be brought to roast at the fire of hell.

16 *at quiet* – "at peace".

17 *I'll devil-porter it no further* – "I'll play the part of the porter of hell-gate no longer" (for the castle is too cold for hell).

18 *the primrose way* is the path of pleasure (as if lined with flowers) which leads to hell (*the everlasting bonfire*).

19 *remember the porter* – "don't forget to give the porter some money (for opening the gate)".

20 *lie so late* – "stop in bed so late".

21 *the second cock* – "the time of the second cock-crow", about 3 o'clock in the morning.

knock. Who 's there, i' the name of Belzebub?[3] – Here 's a
farmer that hanged himself on the expectation of plenty:[4] come
in time;[5] have napkins[6] enough about you;[7] here you 'll sweat   5
for 't.[8] [*Knocking*] Knock, knock. Who 's there, i' the other
devil's name? – 'Faith,[9] here 's an equivocator[10] that could
swear in both the scales against either scale;[11] who committed
treason enough for God's sake,[12] yet could not equivocate to
heaven:[13] O! come in, equivocator. [*Knocking*] Knock, knock,   10
knock. Who 's there? – 'Faith, here 's an English tailor come
hither for stealing out of a French hose:[14] come in, tailor; here
you may roast your goose.[15] [*Knocking*] Knock, knock. Never
at quiet![16] What are you? – But this place is too cold for hell.
I 'll devil-porter it no further:[17] I had thought to have let in   15
some of all professions that go the primrose way[18] to the everlasting bonfire. [*Knocking*] Anon, anon: I pray you, remember
the porter.[19]

[*Opens the gate*

Enter MACDUFF *and* LENOX

MACDUFF

Was it so late, friend, ere you went to bed,
That you do lie so late?[20]   20

PORTER

'Faith, Sir, we were carousing till the second cock;[21]
And drink, Sir, is a great provoker of three things.

MACDUFF

What three things does drink especially provoke?

67

22 *Marry* – "(By the Virgin) Mary", another of the porter's swear-words.

23 *nose-painting*. A drunkard's nose goes red.

24 *an equivocator*, because it works equally well on both sides, provoking and unprovoking, making and marring, etc.

25 *him*, i.e. lechery.

26 *mars* is the opposite of *makes*: "unmakes, spoils".

27 *giving him the lie* – "knocking him down" (because he is too drunk to stand up); but the phrase can also mean "accuse him of lying", and play is made on this in the following lines.

28 *gave thee the lie*, in the sense "knocked *you* down".

29 *i' the very throat o' me*. The porter now takes *lie* to mean "untruth", and is reminded of another expression, "You lie in your throat", i.e. at the very time of speaking.

30 *I requited him for his lie* – "I repaid him (i.e. drink) for his lie". But now the porter's mind returns to knocking down and fighting, and he imagines himself fighting drunkenness. It *took up* his legs once or twice, but he managed to throw it off at last, being too strong for it (lines 34–6).

31 *made a shift to cast him* – "managed to throw him off".

32 *stirring* – "awake, getting up".

33 *Good morrow* – "Good morning".

PORTER

68

PORTER

Marry,[22] Sir, nose-painting,[23] sleep and urine. Lechery, Sir, it
provokes and unprovokes: it provokes the desire, but it takes   25
away the performance. Therefore, much drink may be said to
be an equivocator[24] with lechery: it makes him[25] and it mars[26]
him; it sets him on, and it takes him off; it persuades him, and
disheartens him; makes him stand to, and not stand to: in
conclusion, equivocates him in a sleep, and, giving him the   30
lie,[27] leaves him.

MACDUFF

I believe drink gave thee the lie[28] last night.

PORTER

That it did, Sir, i' the very throat o' me:[29] but I requited him
for his lie;[30] and, I think, being too strong for him, though he   35
took up my legs sometime, yet I made a shift to cast him.[31]

MACDUFF

Is thy master stirring?[32]

Enter MACBETH

Our knocking has awaked him; here he comes.

LENOX

[*To* MACBETH] Good morrow,[33] noble Sir!

MACBETH

                        Good morrow, both!

MACDUFF

Is the king stirring, worthy thane?

34 *timely* – "early".
35 *slipped the hour* – "let the time (arranged for calling) go by".
36 *a joyful trouble* – "a trouble which brings with it pleasure", but still a trouble (*yet 't is one*).

37 *The labour . . . physics pain* – "The labour in which we take delight cures (*physics*) any pain".
38 *I'll make so bold to call* – "I'll be so bold as to call".
39 *limited* – "appointed".
40 *appoint* – "arrange".
41 *where we lay* – "at the place where we slept".

MACBETH

Not yet.   40

MACDUFF

He did command me to call timely[34] on him:
I have almost slipped the hour.[35]

MACBETH

I 'll bring you to him.

MACDUFF

I know this is a joyful trouble[36] to you;
But yet 't is one.

MACBETH

The labour we delight in physics pain.[37]   45
This is the door.

MACDUFF

I 'll make so bold to call.[38]
For 't is my limited[39] service.

[*Exit*

LENOX

Goes the king hence today?

MACBETH

He does: – he did appoint[40] so.

LENOX

The night has been unruly: where we lay,[41]
Our chimneys were blown down; and, as they say,   50

71

42 *dire combustion* – "terrible disturbance".

43 *confused events . . . woeful time* – "events in confusion just now brought into the world (*new hatched*) at this sad time".

44 *The obscure bird* – "The bird of darkness", the owl. Lady Macbeth was startled by the owl, *the fatal bellman* (II.ii.3).

45 *the livelong night* – "the whole length of the night".

46 *feverous* – "having fever".

47 *My young remembrance . . . to it* – "My memory, that of a young man, cannot compare (*parallel*) an equal (*fellow*) to it (i.e. to last night)".

48 *Tongue, nor heart . . . name thee!* – "Neither tongue nor heart can conceive or name you (the horror)".

49 *Confusion.* The murder of the king is a masterpiece of confusion, for order and the rule of law, as embodied in his person, have been destroyed.

50 *sacrilegious murder.* The king's body, which represents order, is a *temple* (line 64) anointed by God; the murderer has broken open this temple, and thus done a sacrilegious crime. (See glossary under *sacrilege*.)

51 *broke ope* – "broken open".

52 *the building*, i.e. the king's body, God's "temple" of order. The image of the temple is so much in the forefront here that Macbeth pretends not to understand what has actually happened; and Lenox does not in fact.

Lamentings heard i' the air; strange screams of death,
And prophesying with accents terrible
Of dire combustion,[42] and confused events,
New hatched to the woeful time.[43]
The obscure bird[44] clamoured the livelong night:[45]   55
Some say the earth was feverous,[46] and did shake.

MACBETH

'T was a rough night.

LENOX

My young remembrance cannot parallel
A fellow to it.[47]

Re-enter MACDUFF

MACDUFF

O horror! horror! horror! Tongue, nor heart,   60
Cannot conceive, nor name thee![48]

MACBETH *and* LENOX

What 's the matter?

MACDUFF

Confusion[49] now hath made his masterpiece!
Most sacrilegious murder[50] hath broke ope[51]
The Lord's anointed temple, and stole thence
The life o' the building![52]

MACBETH

What is 't you say? the life?   65

LENOX

Mean you his majesty?

73

53 *a new Gorgon.* Medusa, one of the Gorgons, was once a beautiful girl, but Athena changed her into a terrible monster. Anyone who looked at her head was blinded and turned to stone. The sight of the king's body is so terrible that its effect might be like that of the Gorgon Medusa (see illustration).

54 *up, up* – "get up".

55 *The great doom's image* – "the image of the last judgement after death, Doomsday".

56 *sprites* – "spirits".

57 *countenance* – "look upon".

58 *a hideous trumpet calls to parley* – "a terrible trumpet calls to meeting". Lady Macbeth compares the bell with a trumpet such as is used on the field of battle to call people together.

a new Gorgon[53]

MACDUFF

Approach the chamber, and destroy your sight
With a new Gorgon.[53] – Do not bid me speak:
See, and then speak yourselves. –

[Exeunt MACBETH *and* LENOX

                    Awake! awake! –
Ring the alarum-bell. – Murder and treason!   70
Banquo and Donalbain! Malcolm! awake!
Shake off this downy sleep, death's counterfeit,
And look on death itself! – up, up,[54] and see
The great doom's image![55] – Malcolm! Banquo!
As from your graves rise up, and walk like sprites[56]   75
To countenance[57] this horror! Ring the bell.

[Bell rings

Enter LADY MACBETH

LADY MACBETH

What's the business,
That such a hideous trumpet calls to parley[58]
The sleepers of the house? speak, speak!

MACDUFF

                    O gentle lady,
'T is not for you to hear what I can speak: 80
The repetition, in a woman's ear,
Would murder as it fell.

Enter BANQUO

             O Banquo! Banquo!
Our royal master 's murdered!

59 *Duff* – "Macduff". *Mac* is a prefix, meaning "son of".
60 *Had I but* – "If only I had".
61 *chance* – "occurrence".
62 *I had lived* – "I should have lived".
63 *The wine of life . . . to brag of* – "The wine of life has been run off (from the cask) (*is drawn*), and only the dregs (*the mere lees*) are left for this vault to boast of." The *wine of life* runs off like blood from the body, and this world (the place where the wine of life is kept, the wine-vault) can boast only about the dregs which have been left behind. But *vault* is extended to mean also the roof of the sky covering the world, and so the world itself. (See glossary under *vault.* [2])

64 *What is amiss?* – "What is wrong?" Macbeth tells Donalbain in answer that he himself is *amiss*, not in a state of well-being, although he does not know it.
65 *The spring, the head, the fountain* all suggest origin, or place of origin, particularly where water comes up from the earth, the *very source* in line 95. Here the *fountain* of blood is connected with the murder and also with the king's fatherhood of the questioner.

76

LADY MACBETH
Woe, alas!
What! in our house?

BANQUO
Too cruel anywhere.
Dear Duff,[59] I pr'ythee, contradict thyself,   85
And say it is not so.

Re-enter MACBETH *and* LENOX

MACBETH
Had I but[60] died an hour before this chance,[61]
I had lived[62] a blessed time; for, from this instant,
There 's nothing serious in mortality;
All is but toys: renown, and grace, is dead;   90
The wine of life is drawn, and the mere lees
Is left this vault to brag of.[63]

Enter MALCOLM *and* DONALBAIN

DONALBAIN
What is amiss?[64]

MACBETH
You are, and do not know 't:
The spring, the head, the fountain[65] of your blood
Is stopped; the very source of it is stopped.   95

MACDUFF
Your royal father 's murdered.

MALCOLM
O! by whom?

66 *badged* – "marked", particularly with bright colours, like a badge.

67 *I do repent me of my fury* – "I am sorry about my anger". In this way Macbeth tells them indirectly that he has killed the two servants who were supposed to be guarding the king.

68 *amazed* – "confused".

69 *Loyal and neutral* – "faithful (to one side in a disagreement) and fair to both sides".

70 *in a moment* – "at the same time". He asks, "Who can, at the same time, be wise *and* confused, . . .?"

71 *expedition* – "speed".

72 *the pauser reason* – "reason, which makes one pause (and think)".

73 *His silver skin . . . golden blood; laced* – "marked with a pattern like lace". The skin of Duncan is *silver* in contrast to the "gold" of his blood.

74 *For ruin's wasteful entrance* – "for the wasteful entrance of ruin", i.e. death, destruction, as a kind of opposite to *nature* – "life", in the line before.

75 *their daggers . . . with gore* – "their daggers horribly clothed in blood"; *breached* is perhaps for *breeched* – "wearing breeches or trousers". Their daggers had "breeches" of blood, which were *unmannerly* ("improper"), for the proper "trousers" for daggers are sheaths.

76 *Who could refrain* (line 113) . . . *love known* – "Who that had a heart, and in that heart courage, could refrain from making his love known?"; i.e. "Is there anybody who has . . .?"

LENOX

Those of his chamber, as it seemed, had done 't:
Their hands and faces were all badged[66] with blood;
So were their daggers, which, unwiped, we found
Upon their pillows: 100
They stared, and were distracted; no man's life
Was to be trusted with them.

MACBETH

O! yet I do repent me of my fury[67]
That I did kill them.

MACDUFF

Wherefore did you so?

MACBETH

Who can be wise, amazed,[68] temperate and furious,   105
Loyal and neutral,[69] in a moment?[70] No man:
The expedition[71] of my violent love
Outran the pauser reason.[72] – Here lay Duncan,
His silver skin laced with his golden blood;[73]
And his gashed stabs looked like a breach in nature   110
For ruin's wasteful entrance:[74] there, the murderers,
Steeped in the colours of their trade, their daggers
Unmannerly breached with gore.[75] Who could refrain,
That had a heart to love, and in that heart
Courage, to make 's love known?[76]

LADY MACBETH

[*Fainting*]   Help me hence, ho!   115

MACDUFF

Look to the lady.

79

77 *Why do we . . . for ours?* – "Why do we (the king's sons), whom this matter (*argument*) touches most closely, remain silent (*hold our tongues*)?"

78 *What should be spoken* – "What can be said".

79 *auger-hole* – "a very small hole"; the fate of the brothers, though so small (and hidden) as to be hardly noticeable, may come out quickly and take them, for their lives too must be in danger.

80 *our tears Are not yet brewed* – "our tears are not yet ready for crying". They feel their sorrow, but realise that this is not the place to show it; for here some of the sorrow expressed seems to be false.

81 *Nor our strong . . . of motion* – "Our sorrow, although strong, (is not yet) ready to move (and therefore show itself)".

82 *when we have . . . hid* – "when we have hidden our undressed bodies (*naked frailties*, dressed only in night-clothes)", i.e. when we have dressed.

83 *question* – "examine".

84 *To know it further* – "so as to get to know more about it".

85 *In the great hand of God*, in His protection.

86 *and thence . . . treasonous malice* – "and from that place (*the great hand of God*) I fight against the plans, unknown as yet (*the undivulged pretence*), of treacherous (*treasonous*) ill-will".

87 *So all* – "So do we all".

MALCOLM

[*Aside to* DONALBAIN] Why do we hold our tongues,
That most may claim this argument for ours?[77]

DONALBAIN

[*Aside to* MALCOLM] What should be spoken[78]
Here where our fate, hid in an auger-hole,[79]   120
May rush and seize us? Let 's away: our tears
Are not yet brewed.[80]

MALCOLM

[*Aside to* DONALBAIN] Nor our strong sorrow
Upon the foot of motion.[81]

BANQUO

Look to the lady: —

[LADY MACBETH *is carried out*

And when we have our naked frailties hid,[82]
That suffer in exposure, let us meet,   125
And question[83] this most bloody piece of work,
To know it further.[84] Fears and scruples shake us:
In the great hand of God[85] I stand; and thence
Against the undivulged pretence I fight
Of treasonous malice.[86]

MACDUFF

And so do I.

ALL

So all.[87]   130

81

88 *briefly* – "quickly".

89 *put on manly readiness* – "dress ourselves, in men's clothes", perhaps in contrast to the night-clothes, which look like women's.

90 *Well contented* – "(We are) very pleased (to do as you suggest)".

91 *consort* – "keep company".

92 *an office* – "a service".

93 *easy* for *easily*.

94 *our separated fortune* – "our chances if we go separately".

95 *the near in blood, The nearer bloody* – "The closer (*near*) one is to a (murdered) person in blood relationship, the nearer one is to a fate which may be bloody".

96 *This murderous shaft . . . lighted* – "This murderous arrow (*shaft*) that has been shot has not yet come to earth (*lighted*)"; the arrow of death, the blow which killed Duncan, is still in the air, and may hit them next.

97 *to horse* – "to our horses".

98 *dainty of leave-taking* – "particular about the way we say goodbye".

99 *shift away* – "move away quickly".

100 *There 's warrant . . . steals itself* – "There is authority (*warrant*) in the kind of thieving which (only) steals itself away". The play is on the word *steal*, meaning both "take illegally" and "go away in secret". If one "steals" away, one is not "stealing" anything.

MACBETH

Let 's briefly[88] put on manly readiness,[89]
And meet i' the hall together.

ALL

Well contented.[90]

[*Exeunt all but* MALCOLM *and* DONALBAIN

MALCOLM

What will you do? Let 's not consort[91] with them:
To show an unfelt sorrow is an office[92]
Which the false man does easy.[93] I 'll to England.   135

DONALBAIN

To Ireland, I: our separated fortune[94]
Shall keep us both the safer; where we are
There 's daggers in men's smiles; the near in blood,
The nearer bloody.[95]

MALCOLM

                    This murderous shaft that 's shot
Hath not yet lighted,[96] and our safest way   140
Is to avoid the aim: therefore, to horse,[97]
And let us not be dainty of leave-taking,[98]
But shift away.[99] There 's warrant in that theft
Which steals itself,[100] when there 's no mercy left.

[*Exeunt*

(II.iv) Rosse talks with an old man about the supernatural events seen round about Macbeth's castle the night before. Macduff comes in from the castle and tells them that, since the king's sons have fled, suspicion naturally falls on them. But he himself is unconvinced. Macbeth, now the strongest man in the kingdom, is the natural choice for a new king, and has gone to be crowned. But Macduff refuses to attend the ceremony.

1 *Threescore and ten* – "Seventy (years)".
2 *volume* – "space".
3 *this sore night . . . knowings* – "this terrible (*sore*) night has made things I can remember (*knowings*) from former times seem small"; *trifled* – "made small by comparison".
4 *the heavens* – "the sky".
5 *as* – "as if".
6 *man's act* – "what men do".
7 *Threatens.* The sky is quite dark, "threatening" the scene.
8 *the travelling lamp* is the sun, which is "strangled" or killed by the darkness.
9 *Is 't night's* (line 8) *. . . should kiss it?* – "Is it (because of) the night's influence (*predominance*) or (because of) the day's shame that darkness buries (*does . . . entomb*) the face of the earth when living light should kiss it?" (The day may be "ashamed" to look on the deed that has been done.)

10 *unnatural*, i.e. bad, because not according to nature, the natural order of the world. It is "natural" for the sun to shine during the day; it is "unnatural" for a man to murder his king.
11 *Even like . . . that 's done* – "just as the deed that has been done (is unnatural)".
12 *towering in her pride of place.* Hunting with falcons was once a popular sport in England. The birds were trained to fly higher and higher in circles when let free (this was called *towering*). When they reached the high point (*the pride of place*), they dropped down at great speed on to the animal they were sent out to kill.
13 *Was by a mousing owl hawked at* – "was attacked (as a hawk attacks) by an owl of the kind which hunts mice". This, too, was unnatural, for the strong falcon should have been able to kill the owl (see illustration p. 86).
14 *Beauteous and swift . . . of their race* – "beautiful (*Beauteous*) and fast-running, the favourites (*minions*) of their kind (*race*)".
15 *broke their stalls* – "broke away from the stalls".
16 *flung out* – "kicked and plunged".
17 *Contending 'gainst obedience* – "fighting against control".
18 *as* – "as if".

Scene IV. Outside the Castle.
Enter ROSSE *and an* OLD MAN.

OLD MAN

Threescore and ten[1] I can remember well;
Within the volume[2] of which time I have seen
Hours dreadful and things strange, but this sore night
Hath trifled former knowings.[3]

ROSSE

                Ha, good father,
Thou seest, the heavens,[4] as[5] troubled with man's act,[6]   5
Threatens[7] his bloody stage: by the clock 't is day,
And yet dark night strangles the travelling lamp.[8]
Is 't night's predominance, or the day's shame,
That darkness does the face of earth entomb,
When living light should kiss it?[9]

OLD MAN

                'T is unnatural,[10]   10
Even like the deed that 's done.[11] On Tuesday last,
A falcon, towering in her pride of place,[12]
Was by a mousing owl hawked at,[13] and killed.

ROSSE

And Duncan's horses (a thing most strange and certain)
Beauteous and swift, the minions of their race,[14]   15
Turned wild in nature, broke their stalls,[15] flung out,[16]
Contending 'gainst obedience,[17] as[18] they would make
War with mankind.

OLD MAN

        'T is said, they ate each other.

19 *Those that Macbeth hath slain* are the chamberlains whose daggers were used for the murder.
20 *Alas, the day!* is a common expression of sorrow; the original meaning was, perhaps, "It is sad that I should have seen the day (on which such a thing has happened)".
21 *pretend* – "intend (to do)".
22 *suborned* – "urged on (to do it)".
23 *Are stol'n away* – "have gone away secretly".

24 *Thriftless Ambition* – "ambition which is not used sparingly", not properly controlled.
25 *ravin up* – "eat up".
26 *Thine own life's means!* – "your own means of life". (He is addressing Ambition.) Rosse takes it that the king has been killed by his sons; he is their *life's means*, and their ambition has consequently destroyed its own origin.
27 *like* – "likely (that)".
28 *sovereignty* – "kingship".

ROSSE

They did so, to th' amazement of mine eyes,
That looked upon 't –

Enter MACDUFF

                    Here comes the good Macduff. –   20
How goes the world, Sir, now?

MACDUFF

                    Why, see you not?

ROSSE

Is 't known, who did this more than bloody deed?

MACDUFF

Those that Macbeth hath slain.[19]

ROSSE

                    Alas, the day![20]
What good could they pretend?[21]

MACDUFF

                    They were suborned.[22]
Malcolm and Donalbain, the king's two sons,   25
Are stol'n away[23] and fled; which puts upon them
Suspicion of the deed.

ROSSE

                    'Gainst nature still:
Thriftless Ambition,[24] that wilt ravin up[25]
Thine own life's means![26] – Then 't is most like[27]
The sovereignty[28] will fall upon Macbeth.   30

29 *named* – "named as king".
30 *Scone.* This town, once the capital of Scotland, was the crowning-place of the Scottish kings.
31 *invested* – "made king, robed in the clothes of kingship".
32 *Colme-kill*, a small island off the west coast of Scotland, was the historical burial-place of the kings of Scotland. It is now called Iona.
33 *Will you to Scone?* – "Do you intend to go to Scone?"

34 *Fife* is a district (now a county) of Scotland.
35 *Lest our old robes . . . our new!* – "In case our old clothes fit us better than our new ones"; i.e. in case the old times suit us better than the times to come.
36 *father*, used as a form of address to any old man.
37 *benison* – "blessing".
38 *with those That would* – "with (all) those who want to . . ."

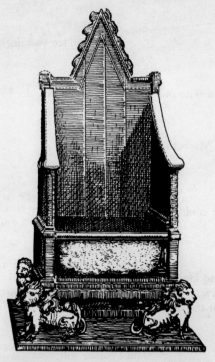

gone to Scone³⁰

To be invested³¹

MACDUFF

He is already named,[29] and gone to Scone[30]
To be invested.[31]

ROSSE

Where is Duncan's body?

MACDUFF

Carried to Colme-kill,[32]
The sacred storehouse of his predecessors,
And guardian of their bones.

ROSSE

Will you to Scone?[33]   35

MACDUFF

No, cousin; I 'll to Fife.[34]

ROSSE

Well, I will thither.

MACDUFF

Well, may you see things well done there: – adieu! –
Lest our old robes sit easier than our new![35]

ROSSE

Farewell, father.[36]

OLD MAN

God's benison[37] go with you; and with those   40
That would[38] make good of bad, and friends of foes!

[*Exeunt*

(III.i) Banquo, now back in the royal castle of Forres, is also suspicious of Macbeth, but remembers that what has happened is a fulfilment of the witches' prophecies, and that these were favourable towards him. Macbeth and his wife come in as king and queen of Scotland, and tell him that he will be their guest of honour at the feast that evening. Macbeth finds out from Banquo that he plans to be away from the castle all day, and will probably not be back until after nightfall; Fleance is to go with him.

By arrangement, two wretched soldiers are waiting to see Macbeth; he has already told them something of what he wants, and he now explains further. He pretends to them that Banquo has long been their secret enemy and the cause of their bad fortune, and now he wants them to murder him and his son Fleance. Banquo is, in fact, a danger to him both because he is famous for nobility of character and also because the witches have foretold for his descendants a line of kings.

1 *Thou*. Banquo is talking about Macbeth, and addressing his words to him as if he were there.

2 *Thou playedst . . . for 't* – "you acted most wickedly for it".

3 *stand in thy posterity* – "pass on to your children".

4 *myself* for *I myself*.

5 *root*. Noble families and some others have "family trees", in which the descent of the family is shown in the form of branches on a tree. The witches foretold that Banquo would be the beginning, the *root* of such a tree.

6 *them*, the weird women.

7 *their speeches shine* – "their words show favour".

8 *the verities on thee made good* – "the truths which have been proved in your case".

9 *be my oracles as well* – "tell me also what will happen in the future". (See *oracle* in the glossary.)

10 *Sennet* – "Signal call" on a trumpet, sounded to tell that the king is coming.

11 *our chief guest*, Banquo, whom both Macbeth and his wife now begin to treat with special favour.

12 *It had been* – "it would have been".

13 *all-thing* – "absolutely".

14 *solemn* – "formal".

90

ACT THREE

Scene I. Forres. A room in the palace.
Enter BANQUO

BANQUO

Thou[1] hast it now, King, Cawdor, Glamis, all,
As the weird women promised; and, I fear,
Thou playedst most foully for 't;[2] yet it was said,
It should not stand in thy posterity;[3]
But that myself[4] should be the root[5] and father   5
Of many kings. If there come truth from them[6]
(As upon thee, Macbeth, their speeches shine[7]),
Why, by the verities on thee made good,[8]
May they not be my oracles as well,[9]
And set me up in hope? But, hush; no more.   10

Sennet[10] *sounded. Enter* MACBETH *as King*;
LADY MACBETH *as Queen*; LENOX, ROSSE,
Lords, *and* Attendants.

MACBETH

Here 's our chief guest.[11]

LADY MACBETH

                    If he had been forgotten,
It had been[12] as a gap in our great feast,
And all-thing[13] unbecoming.

MACBETH

[*To* BANQUO] Tonight we hold a solemn[14] supper, Sir,
And I 'll request your presence.

91

15 *Let your highness* (line 15) . . . *For ever knit* – "Command me, your highness, and my duties are tied (*knit*) to that command with a bond (*tie*) which can never be broken".

16 *We should have else desired* – "I should otherwise have asked for . . ." (but I cannot now, because you are riding away).

17 *Which still . . . grave and prosperous* – "which has always been both responsible (*grave*) and profitable (*prosperous*)".

18 *go not my horse the better* – "if my horse does not go more quickly (than I expect)".

19 *I must become . . . or twain* – "I shall have to take one or two (*twain*) hours of darkness from the night", ride for an hour or two after dark.

20 *Fail not* – "Do not miss".

21 *our bloody cousins*, Malcolm and Donalbain, who are, through their father, relatives (*cousins*) to Macbeth. He calls them *bloody* in an attempt to make people believe that it was they who murdered Duncan.

22 *bestowed* – "settled".

23 *filling their hearers With strange invention* – "(and) filling the ears of those who listen to them with strange ideas that they have invented". They have begun talking about their suspicions of Macbeth.

24 *of that tomorrow* – "(Let us talk) about that tomorrow".

BANQUO

                    Let your highness   15
Command upon me, to the which my duties
Are with a most indissoluble tie
For ever knit.[15]

MACBETH

Ride you this afternoon?

BANQUO

             Ay, my good lord.

MACBETH

We should have else desired[16] your good advice   20
(Which still hath been both grave and prosperous)[17]
In this day's council; but we 'll take tomorrow.
Is 't far you ride?

BANQUO

As far, my lord, as will fill up the time
'Twixt this and supper: go not my horse the better,[18]   25
I must become a borrower of the night
For a dark hour or twain.[19]

MACBETH

             Fail not[20] our feast.

BANQUO

My lord, I will not.

MACBETH

We hear our bloody cousins[21] are bestowed[22]
In England and in Ireland; not confessing   30
Their cruel parricide, filling their hearers
With strange invention.[23] But of that tomorrow,[24]

25 *therewithal* – "along with it".

26 *cause of state Craving us jointly* – "matters of state which will need (the attention of) both of us together". Macbeth is now doing all he can to win Banquo's confidence, and to keep it.

27 *Hie you to horse* – "Go quickly to your horse."

28 *our time does call upon 's* – "this occasion demands us both".

29 *sure of foot* – "sure-footed", firm in movement on the ground.

30 *to make . . . welcome* – "in order to make company (*society*) more delightful and welcome".

31 *while* – "until".

32 *Sirrah* is a form of *Sir*, used in addressing servants, etc.

33 *Attend those men Our pleasure?* – "Are those men waiting (until) I wish (to see them)?"

34 *without* – "outside".

35 *To be thus . . . safely thus* – "It is nothing to be like this (i.e. a king) unless one can be it (a king) in safety".

36 *in his royalty . . . would be feared* – "that thing which would naturally be feared reigns in his natural nobility (*royalty of nature*)". It is simply that Macbeth, the bad, fears Banquo, the good.

37 *'t is much he dares* – "he dares do a great deal"; he is not only good but brave.

38 *to that dauntless . . . his mind* – "in addition to that brave disposition of his character".

When, therewithal,[25] we shall have cause of state
Craving us jointly.[26] Hie you to horse;[27] adieu,
Till you return at night. Goes Fleance with you?   35

BANQUO

Ay, my good lord: our time does call upon 's.[28]

MACBETH

I wish your horses swift, and sure of foot;[29]
And so I do commend you to their backs.
Farewell. –

                                 [*Exit* BANQUO

[*To the Lords*] Let every man be master of his time   40
Till seven at night; to make society
The sweeter welcome,[30] we will keep ourself
Till supper-time alone: while[31] then, God be with you.

                    [*Exeunt* LADY MACBETH, Lords, *etc.*

[*To an* Attendant] Sirrah,[32] a word with you. Attend those
   men
Our pleasure?[33]   45

ATTENDANT

They are, my lord, without[34] the palace gate.

MACBETH

Bring them before us. [*Exit* Attendant] – To be thus is nothing,
But to be safely thus.[35] – Our fears in Banquo
Stick deep, and in his royalty of nature
Reigns that which would be feared;[36] 't is much he dares;[37]   50
And, to that dauntless temper of his mind,[38]
He hath a wisdom that doth guide his valour
To act in safety. There is none but he

39 *being* – "existence".

40 *My genius is rebuked* – "My guardian spirit is overcome", because it is too weak to resist Banquo's good angel.

41 *Caesar.* Shakespeare's *Julius Caesar* in part deals with this relationship between Caesar and Antony.

42 *He chid the sisters* – "He rebuked the (weird) sisters". But it is not true that Banquo *chid* them, though Macbeth would like to think he did; Banquo wanted to know his own future, but said, "(I) neither beg nor fear Your favours nor your hate". (I.iii.60–1).

43 *a fruitless crown* – "a kingship not bearing fruit", the crown of a king whose children would not be kings after him. The *sceptre*, also a sign of kingship, is described in the following line as *barren*, "childless".

44 *gripe* for *grip*.

45 *Thence to be . . . unlineal hand* – ". . . (only) to be pulled away (out of my grip) by the hand of one who is not a descendant of mine (*unlineal*)".

46 *For Banquo's . . . filed my mind* – "I have defiled (*filed*) my mind on behalf of Banquo's children (not my own)".

47 *Put rancours . . . of my peace.* The image here is of Macbeth's peace of mind as a vessel, say a drinking vessel; *rancours* are things in food or drink which are bitter because not fresh. The vessel of peace now contains bitter drink.

48 *mine eternal jewel* – "my soul", the most precious part of me, the part which is indestructible.

49 *the common enemy of man* – "the devil, Satan".

50 *list* – "place of battle".

51 *champion me* – "be my champion; stand by me as my supporter".

52 *to the utterance* – "to the finish".

53 *so please your highness* – "if it pleases your highness (for me to say so)".

54 *considered of* – "thought about".

55 *my speeches* – "the things I told (you)".

56 *he* – Banquo.

57 *which* – "who".

58 *So under fortune* – "in such a miserable state".

sceptre

Whose being[39] I do fear: and under him
My genius is rebuked,[40] as, it is said,   55
Mark Antony's was by Caesar.[41] He chid the sisters[42]
When first they put the name of king upon me,
And bade them speak to him; then, prophet-like,
They hailed him father to a line of kings.
Upon my head they placed a fruitless crown,[43]   60
And put a barren sceptre in my gripe,[44]
Thence to be wrenched with an unlineal hand,[45]
No son of mine succeeding. If 't be so,
For Banquo's issue have I filed my mind;[46]
For them the gracious Duncan have I murdered;   65
Put rancours in the vessel of my peace[47]
Only for them; and mine eternal jewel[48]
Given to the common enemy of man,[49]
To make them kings, the seed of Banquo kings!
Rather than so, come, fate, into the list,[50]   70
And champion me[51] to the utterance![52] – Who 's there? –

Re-enter Attendant, *with two* Murderers

[*To the* Attendant] Now, go to the door, and stay there till we
     call.

                                              [*Exit* Attendant

[*To the* Murderers] Was it not yesterday we spoke together?

I MURDERER

It was, so please your highness.[53]

MACBETH
                         Well then, now
Have you considered of[54] my speeches?[55] Know   75
That it was he,[56] in the times past, which[57] held you
So under fortune,[58] which, you thought, had been

59 *which, you thought . . . innocent self* – "and you thought that this (person, who had brought you to such a miserable state) had been *I*, who am innocent (of any such thing) (*our innocent self*)". Macbeth is trying to persuade the murderers that their misfortunes are due to Banquo, not himself, and is hoping that they may conceive a hatred for Banquo, and be brought to murder him.

60 *made good to you* – "proved to you".

61 *passed in probation with you* – "convinced you by proof".

62 *borne in hand* – "deceived".

63 *how crossed* – "how (you were) hindered (in what you planned to do)".

64 *the instruments* – "(by) what means (you were hindered)".

65 *Who wrought with them* – "who it was who worked (by these means)".

66 *and all things* (line 81) . . . *did Banquo* – "and everything else, which would tell (a man with even) half a soul and a weak mind (*a notion crazed*), 'Banquo did this'".

67 *Our point of second meeting* – "the point of our second meeting".

68 *gospelled* – "filled with the (Christian) teaching of the Gospels", which requires a man to pray even for his enemies.

69 *To pray* – "as to pray".

70 *his issue* – "his children and descendants"; Macbeth's thoughts naturally turn to them, for they are fated to be kings.

71 *yours* – "your people".

72 *We are men*, i.e. only human beings, and therefore able to bear only a certain amount of ill-usage.

73 *my liege* – "my lord".

74 *in the catalogue* – "in the list (of things in nature)"; there they are certainly included under the general term "men". But there are many kinds of men as there are many kinds of dog.

75 *Shoughs* – "rough-haired dogs".

76 *water-rugs* – (perhaps) "long-haired dogs living by the water".

77 *demi-wolves* – "half-wolves", dogs bred from wolves and dogs.

78 *are clept All* – "are all called".

79 *the valued file* – "the list which gives the comparative values (of dogs)".

80 *Hath in him closed* – "has placed in him".

81 *he does receive Particular addition* – "he receives (from us) an additional name, according to his qualities".

82 *the bill That writes them all alike* is the list which calls them all dogs, unlike the *valued file* in line 94.

83 *a station in the file* – "a place in that list".

Our innocent self.[59] This I made good to you[60]
In our last conference; passed in probation with you[61]
How you were borne in hand;[62] how crossed;[63] the
    instruments;[64]   80
Who wrought with them;[65] and all things else, that might
To half a soul, and to a notion crazed,
Say, "Thus did Banquo".[66]

I MURDERER

    You made it known to us.

MACBETH

I did so; and went further, which is now
Our point of second meeting.[67] Do you find   85
Your patience so predominant in your nature
That you can let this go? Are you so gospelled[68]
To pray[69] for this good man, and for his issue,[70]
Whose heavy hand hath bowed you to the grave
And beggared yours[71] for ever?

I MURDERER

    We are men,[72] my liege.[73]   90

MACBETH

Ay, in the catalogue[74] ye go for men;
As hounds and greyhounds, mongrels, spaniels, curs,
Shoughs,[75] water-rugs,[76] and demi-wolves[77] are clept
All[78] by the name of dogs: the valued file[79]
Distinguishes the swift, the slow, the subtle,   95
The housekeeper, the hunter, every one
According to the gift which bounteous nature
Hath in him closed;[80] whereby he does receive
Particular addition,[81] from the bill
That writes them all alike;[82] and so of men.   100
Now, if you have a station in the file,[83]
Not i' the worst rank of manhood, say it;

84 *bosoms* – "hearts, minds".

85 *Whose execution takes your enemy off* – "the carrying out of which (business) will remove your enemy".

86 *Grapples you . . . love of us* – "will bind (*Grapples*) you to me in heart and love".

87 *Who wear . . . in his life* – "(I) who am only 'poor in health' (i.e. have no feeling of security) so long as he lives".

88 *Which in . . . perfect* – "(my health), which would be perfect if he were dead".

89 *I am reckless* – "I do not care".

90 *tugged with fortune* – "roughly handled by chance".

91 *To mend it* – "to make it (my life) better."

92 *be rid on 't* – "be free of it".

93 *in such bloody distance* – "with such bitter hatred".

94 *every minute . . . near'st of life* – "every minute of his existence (*being*) presses into the most essential parts of my body (*my near'st of life*)". The thought of Banquo living gives him bodily pain.

95 *bare-faced power* – "power openly shown".

96 *And bid my will avouch it* – "and tell my mind that it was the right thing to do".

97 *For* – "because of".

98 *Whose loves I may not drop* – "whose love (the *certain friends*') I cannot (afford to) lose".

99 *but wail . . . struck down* – "but (I must) show sorrow for (*wail*) the death (*fall*) of the man I killed myself".

100 *thence* – "so".

And I will put that business in your bosoms,[84]
Whose execution takes your enemy off,[85]
Grapples you to the heart and love of us,[86]   105
Who wear our health but sickly in his life,[87]
Which in his death were perfect.[88]

2 MURDERER

               I am one, my liege.
Whom the vile blows and buffets of the world
Have so incensed, that I am reckless[89] what
I do to spite the world.

1 MURDERER

            And I another,   110
So weary with disasters, tugged with fortune,[90]
That I would set my life on any chance
To mend it[91] or be rid on 't.[92]

MACBETH

            Both of you
Know Banquo was your enemy.

BOTH MURDERERS

            True, my lord.

MACBETH

So is he mine; and in such bloody distance[93]   115
That every minute of his being thrusts
Against my near'st of life;[94] and though I could
With bare-faced power[95] sweep him from my sight,
And bid my will avouch it,[96] yet I must not,
For[97] certain friends, that are both his and mine,   120
Whose loves I may not drop,[98] but wail his fall
Who I myself struck down:[99] and thence[100] it is
That I to your assistance do make love,

101 *Masking* – "covering up".
102 *the common eye* – "the sight of everyone".
103 *sundry* – "various".
104 *Though our lives* – The Murderer is doubtless going to say something to the effect, "(We shall do it even) though our lives depended on it", but Macbeth interrupts him; he is in a hurry to complete the agreement.
105 *Your spirits shine through you.* He can see they are trustworthy, and will do what they promise.
106 *at most* – "at the latest".
107 *plant* – "hide".

108 *the perfect . . . moment on 't* – "the exact information, obtained by spying, as to the best time, the (right) moment for it (the deed)".
109 *something from the palace* – "some distance away from the castle".
110 *always thought . . . a clearness* – "remembering always that I must have (my house) clear (of the deed)".
111 *rubs* – "faults".
112 *absence* is a way of saying "death".
113 *Resolve yourselves apart* – "(Go to) one side (*apart*), and make up your minds".
114 *straight* – "at once".

Masking[101] the business from the common eye,[102]
For sundry[103] weighty reasons.

2 MURDERER

                    We shall, my lord,   125
Perform what you command us.

1 MURDERER

                    Though our lives —[104]

MACBETH

Your spirits shine through you.[105] Within this hour at most[106]
I will advise you where to plant[107] yourselves,
Acquaint you with the perfect spy o' the time,
The moment on 't,[108] for 't must be done tonight   130
And something from the palace;[109] always thought
That I require a clearness:[110] and with him
(To leave no rubs,[111] nor botches, in the work),
Fleance his son, that keeps him company,
Whose absence[112] is no less material to me   135
Than is his father's, must embrace the fate
Of that dark hour. Resolve yourselves apart;[113]
I 'll come to you anon.

2 MURDERER

We are resolved, my lord.

MACBETH

I 'll call upon you straight:[114] abide within. —

                                        [*Exeunt* Murderers

It is concluded: Banquo, thy soul's flight,   140
If it find heaven, must find it out tonight.

                                        [*Exit*

(III.ii) Macbeth and his wife, with a quick understanding beyond words, hint at the need to them of the murder of Banquo. But this time Lady Macbeth is less purposeful and Macbeth determines to keep from her the details of his plan.

1 *Nought 's had . . . without content* – "Nothing is gained, everything is lost (*spent*), when what we have wished for (*our desire*) is got without bringing happiness."

2 *How now* – "How (are you) now? What news now?"

3 *Of sorriest . . . making* – "making, as your companions, the most miserable (*sorriest*) thoughts".

4 *Using* – "using (as companions)".

5 *all* – "any".

6 *without regard* – "not thought of".

Scene II. The same. Another room.

Enter LADY MACBETH *and a* Servant.

LADY MACBETH

Is Banquo gone from court?

SERVANT

Ay, Madam, but returns again tonight.

LADY MACBETH

Say to the king, I would attend his leisure
For a few words.

SERVANT

Madam, I will.

[*Exit*

LADY MACBETH

                    Nought 's had, all 's spent,
Where our desire is got without content:[1]   5
'T is safer to be that which we destroy,
Than by destruction dwell in doubtful joy.

Enter MACBETH

How now,[2] my lord? Why do you keep alone,
Of sorriest fancies your companions making,[3]
Using[4] those thoughts which should indeed have died   10
With them they think on? Things without all[5] remedy
Should be without regard:[6] what 's done is done.

7 *scotched* – "cut, wounded". The snake is an image for the forces which are opposing Macbeth in his rise to power. Although Duncan is dead, there are his sons to consider, and Banquo and Fleance, all in some way connected with kingship.

8 *She 'll close* – "she (the snake) will heal, come together again."

9 *her former tooth* – "her bite as it was before (she was cut)".

10 *But let the frame . . . suffer, Ere we . . .* The meaning of this line is uncertain. Perhaps it is: "But let earth and heaven (*the frame of things,* the frame of the universe) fall to pieces, let (our life in) both this world and the next suffer, before we. . . ."

11 *eat our meal in fear* – "live in fear".

12 *shake us* – "make us shake (with fear)".

13 *Better be* – "It is better to be".

14 *place* – "position (as king)".

15 *sent to peace* – "killed", sent to the peace of death.

16 *his worst* – "its (treason's) worst", that a subject should murder his own king.

17 *nor* – "neither".

18 *Malice domestic,* domestic malice, ill-will in his own country.

19 *foreign levy* – "an enforced army from abroad".

20 *Gentle my lord* for "My gentle lord".

21 *sleek o'er* – "smooth over".

22 *Present him eminence* – "Give him the highest honour (at the feast)".

23 *with eye and tongue* – "by the way you look at him and speak to him".

24 *Unsafe the while, that* – "(We are) for the time being unsafe, so that . . ."

25 *we Must lave . . . flattering streams* – "We must wash (*lave*) (our own) honours in these streams of flattery (for Banquo)".

26 *vizards* – "steel face-pieces", used by soldiers in the Middle Ages to protect their faces. Macbeth wishes their faces to be like steel, covering up what they feel in their hearts (see illustration).

27 *scorpions.* His mind, he says, is full of fears, which are like terrible creatures eating into it.

28 *lives* for *live.*

vizards[26]

MACBETH

We have scotched[7] the snake, not killed it:
She 'll close[8] and be herself; whilst our poor malice
Remains in danger of her former tooth.[9]   15
But let the frame of things disjoint, both the worlds suffer,[10]
Ere we will eat our meal in fear,[11] and sleep
In the affliction of these terrible dreams
That shake us[12] nightly. Better be[13] with the dead
Whom we, to gain our place,[14] have sent to peace,[15]   20
Than on the torture of the mind to lie
In restless ecstasy. Duncan is in his grave;
After life's fitful fever he sleeps well;
Treason has done his worst:[16] nor[17] steel, nor poison,
Malice domestic,[18] foreign levy,[19] nothing   25
Can touch him further.

LADY MACBETH

     Come on;
Gentle my lord,[20] sleek o'er[21] your rugged looks;
Be bright and jovial among your guests tonight.

MACBETH

So shall I, love; and so, I pray, be you.
Let your remembrance apply to Banquo: 30
Present him eminence,[22] both with eye and tongue:[23]
Unsafe the while, that[24] we
Must lave our honours in these flattering streams,[25]
And make our faces vizards[26] to our hearts,
Disguising what they are.

LADY MACBETH

     You must leave this.   35

MACBETH

O! full of scorpions[27] is my mind, dear wife!
Thou know'st that Banquo and his Fleance lives.[28]

29 *nature's copy 's not eterne* – "the human body (the 'copy of nature') is not everlasting (*eterne*)".

But *copy* is used at the same time to suggest *copyhold*, the holding of land forming part of a large estate for the period of a holder's life. Thus nature is taken as lord of a large estate; Banquo and Fleance hold the *copy*, or agreement with Nature for the period of their life. "The 'copyhold' given by nature (to Fleance and Banquo) does not last forever (but only for the period of their life)."

30 *jocund* – "joyful".

31 *ere to black Hecate's* (line 41) . . . *yawning peal* – "Before the shard-born beetle has rung the yawning peal of night with his drowsy humming, at the call (*summons*) of black Hecate, the goddess of witchcraft"; *shard-born* – "born in dung".

32 *of dreadful note* – "noteworthy and terrible".

33 *chuck* – "chick", a playful word used in addressing a woman.

34 *Till thou applaud the deed* – "until you praise the thing which has been done".

35 *seeling* was sewing up the eye-lids of a bird, e.g. the falcon, while it was being trained for hunting. It could then fly only as directed, and not in any way it wished. Night "seels" the eyes of men by keeping them in darkness.

36 *Scarf up* – "cover up", as with a cloth.

37 *Cancel, and tear . . . bond.* A bond is an agreement which is binding to both sides; in this case it refers to Banquo's bond of life, that which binds Banquo to life. And, as if it were written on paper, Macbeth prays Night to cancel it and tear it to pieces.

38 *pale* – "white with fear".

39 *Makes wing* – "flies away".

40 *the rooky wood* – "the wood where birds settle for the night".

41 *night's black agents* – "wicked beings that act in the night".

42 *Thou marvellest at* – "You are surprised at".

43 *hold thee still* – "do not be anxious".

44 *make strong themselves* – "make themselves strong".

LADY MACBETH

But in them nature's copy 's not eterne.[29]

MACBETH

There 's comfort yet; they are assailable:
Then be thou jocund.[30] Ere the bat hath flown   40
His cloistered flight; ere to black Hecate's summons
The shard-born beetle, with his drowsy hums,
Hath run night's yawning peal,[31]
There shall be done a deed of dreadful note.[32]

LADY MACBETH

What 's to be done?   45

MACBETH

Be innocent of the knowledge, dearest chuck,[33]
Till thou applaud the deed.[34] Come, seeling[35] Night,
Scarf up[36] the tender eye of pitiful day,
And, with thy bloody and invisible hand,
Cancel, and tear to pieces, that great bond[37]   50
Which keeps me pale![38] – light thickens; and the crow
Makes wing[39] to the rooky wood;[40]
Good things of day begin to droop and drowse,
Whiles night's black agents[41] to their preys do rouse.
Thou marvellest at[42] my words: but hold thee still;[43]   55
Things bad begun make strong themselves[44] by ill.
So, pr'ythee, go with me.

[*Exeunt*

(III.iii) In the twilight the two murderers stand ready with a third man at the castle gate. They hear the sound of horses and then Banquo's voice, as he dismounts and begins to walk up to the castle gate. They set upon him and kill him, but Fleance escapes.

1 *A park* is an enclosed piece of ground with grass and trees growing on it. This scene is laid in the castle park of Forres.

2 *who did . . . with us?* – "who told you to join us?"

3 *He needs not our mistrust* – "There is no need for us to mistrust him (the third murderer)."

4 *since he delivers Our offices* – "since he tells (us that he knows) our work".

5 *To the direction just* – "even to the last detail of our instructions".

6 *yet* – "still".

7 *lated* for *belated* – "coming late, particularly after nightfall".

8 *apace* – "quickly". The traveller spurs his horse on quickly.

9 *To gain the timely inn* – "to reach an inn in good time".

10 *The subject of our watch* – "what we are watching and waiting for".

11 *ho!* is a cry to call people's attention to the speaker.

12 *the note of expectation* – "the list of the guests expected"; as all the other guests expected are in the court, this must be Banquo.

Scene III. The same.

A park,[1] with a road leading to the palace.

Enter three Murderers.

1 MURDERER

But who did bid thee join with us?[2]

3 MURDERER

                Macbeth.

2 MURDERER

He needs not our mistrust,[3] since he delivers
Our offices,[4] and what we have to do,
To the direction just.[5]

1 MURDERER

          Then stand with us.
The west yet[6] glimmers with some streaks of day: 5
Now spurs the lated[7] traveller apace,[8]
To gain the timely inn;[9] and near approaches
The subject of our watch.[10]

3 MURDERER

            Hark, I hear horses.

BANQUO

[*Within*] Give us a light there, ho![11]

2 MURDERER

                Then 't is he; the rest
That are within the note of expectation[12]   10
Already are i' the court.

13 *go about* – "turn back".

14 *Almost a mile*, i.e. away from the castle.

15 *but he does usually . . . their walk* – "but he is doing what people usually do, (namely) walk (not ride) from here to the palace gate".

16 *Stand to 't* – "Ready!"

17 *Let it come down*, both the rain (which Banquo has just mentioned in conversation with Fleance) and the blow which is to kill him.

18 *Thou mayest revenge* – "You may take revenge (on the murderers)".

1 MURDERER

His horses go about.[13]

3 MURDERER

Almost a mile,[14] but he does usually,
So all men do, from hence to the palace gate
Make it their walk.[15]

Enter BANQUO, *and* FLEANCE, *with a torch.*

2 MURDERER

A light, a light!

3 MURDERER

'T is he.

1 MURDERER

Stand to 't.[16]   15

BANQUO

[*To* FLEANCE] It will be rain tonight.

1 MURDERER

Let it come down.[17]

[*The* First Murderer *strikes out the light
while the others assault* BANQUO

BANQUO

O, treachery! Fly, good Fleance, fly, fly, fly!
Thou mayest revenge[18] – [*To the* Murderer] O slave!

[*Dies.* FLEANCE *escapes*

113

19 *Was 't not the way?* – "Was it not
the right way?", the way they had
already agreed upon. The third
murderer seems not to have expected that the light would be
struck out.

(III.iv) The banquet is laid ready in a
great room of the castle, and the
new king and queen welcome their
guests. One of the murderers comes
to a side door and tells Macbeth in
a whisper that Banquo is dead but
Fleance has escaped. Macbeth's wife
calls him back to the entertainment,
and he again greets his guests, re-
gretting only that Banquo is not
among them. The ghost of Banquo
appears and sits in Macbeth's place,
so that when he is asked to sit down
he thinks the table is full. But none
of the others can see the ghost, and
when Macbeth addresses it in horror they think he has been seized by
a fit. Lady Macbeth makes excuses
for him and the ghost disappears.
He proposes a toast to Banquo;
the ghost reappears and Macbeth
is so appalled that the feast cannot
continue and the guests are asked
to leave. Alone together, Macbeth
and his wife spend little time in
talking of Banquo, but their attention turns to Macduff, who seems
to be refusing to obey the new
king's commands.

1 *A room of state* – "A great guest
room".
2 *You know ... sit down* – "You
know your own social ranks
(*degrees*); sit down (in accordance
with them)", i.e. with the highest
at the head of the table.
3 *at first and last* – "from beginning
to end".
4 *Ourself* – "I myself".
5 *with society* – "with the company
present".
6 *play the humble host* – "play the
part of the humble host", and not
remain in his chair of state.
7 *keeps her state* – "stays in her chair
of state" (see illustration).
8 *in best time* – "in good time; later
on".
9 *require her welcome* – "beg her to
welcome you", by mixing with
the company.

her state[7]

114

3 MURDERER

Who did strike out the light?

1 MURDERER

Was 't not the way?[19]

3 MURDERER

There 's but one down: the son is fled.

2 MURDERER

We have lost   20
Best half of our affair.

1 MURDERER

Well, let 's away, and say how much is done.

[*Exeunt*

Scene IV. A room of state[1] *in the palace.*
A banquet prepared. Enter MACBETH, LADY MACBETH,
ROSSE, LENOX, Lords, *and* Attendants.

MACBETH

You know your own degrees, sit down:[2] at first and last,[3]
The hearty welcome.

LORDS

Thanks to your majesty.

MACBETH

Ourself[4] will mingle with society,[5]
And play the humble host.[6]
Our hostess keeps her state,[7] but in best time[8]   5
We will require her welcome.[9]

10 *to the door*, i.e. he comes on to the stage, but remains at the side. Macbeth, attending to the solemn supper he is giving, does not notice the murderer at first, but moves over later to hear a report of the murder of Banquo.

11 *Both sides are even.* There are equal numbers of people sitting on either side of the table; Macbeth goes to sit in the middle.

12 *Be large in mirth* – "Be generous in good cheer".

13 *we'll drink . . . table round* – "we'll drink a cup (of wine) round the table"; passing it from one to the other (see illustration).

14 *'T is better . . . he within* – "It (the blood) is better outside *you* than inside *him*".

15 *despatched* – "killed, sent out of this world".

16 *the like* – "the same".

17 *the nonpareil* – "the one without an equal".

18 *is 'scaped* – "has escaped".

we'll drink a measure[13]

LADY MACBETH

Pronounce it for me, Sir, to all our friends;
For my heart speaks, they are welcome.

Enter First Murderer *to the door.*[10]

MACBETH

[*To* LADY MACBETH] See, they encounter thee with their
  hearts' thanks.
[*To the Company*] Both sides are even:[11] here I 'll sit i' the midst.   10
Be large in mirth;[12] anon, we 'll drink a measure
The table round.[13] [*To the* Murderer] There 's blood upon thy
  face.

MURDERER

'T is Banquo's then.

MACBETH

'T is better thee without, than he within.[14]
Is he despatched?[15]   15

MURDERER

My lord, his throat is cut; that I did for him.

MACBETH

Thou art the best o' the cut-throats; yet he 's good
That did the like[16] for Fleance: if thou didst it,
Thou art the nonpareil.[17]

MURDERER

Most royal Sir,
Fleance is 'scaped.[18]   20

117

19 *my fit* – "my sudden feeling (of doubt and fear)".

20 *I had else been perfect* – "otherwise I should have been in a perfect state, completely successful".

21 *founded* – "firm".

22 *general*, free to go and act where he wishes, as the air which closes round us (*casing*) is free.

23 *cribbed* – "shut in a small space".

24 *saucy doubts* – "doubts breaking in where they are not wanted".

25 *bides* – "rests".

26 *The least a death to nature* – "the smallest being enough to kill any living thing."

27 *grown* – "grown-up".

28 *Hath nature that . . . the present* – "has life (*nature*) that will breed venom in time, but no teeth for the present".

29 *We'll hear ourselves again* – "I'll hear (your news) again when I am by myself".

30 *the cheer* – "the toast".

31 *the feast is sold* (line 33) . . . *with welcome* – "the feast is sold (not given) when it is not frequently declared while it is being eaten (*while 't is a-making*) that it is given cheerfully (*with welcome*)". It was the custom to welcome guests with frequent toasts and declarations of greeting.

32 *To feed . . . at home* – "It would be better to eat at home (than come to that sort of feast)".

33 *From thence*, i.e. away from home.

34 *the sauce . . . is ceremony* – "it is proper courtly behaviour at meal-times (*ceremony*) which is the (true) sauce to food (*meat*)".

35 *Meeting were bare without it* – "coming together (for a feast) would be empty without it (this *ceremony*)".

36 *remembrancer* – "one who reminds".

37 *wait on* – "attend on, go with".

MACBETH

[*Aside*] Then comes my fit[19] again: I had else been perfect;[20]
Whole as the marble, founded[21] as the rock,
As broad and general[22] as the casing air:
But now I am cabined, cribbed,[23] confined, bound in
To saucy doubts[24] and fears. – [*To the* Murderer] But Banquo's
    safe?   25

MURDERER

Ay, my good lord, safe in a ditch he bides,[25]
With twenty trenchèd gashes on his head,
The least a death to nature.[26]

MACBETH

        Thanks for that. –
[*Aside*] There the grown[27] serpent lies: the worm, that 's fled,
Hath nature that in time will venom breed,
No teeth for the present.[28] – [*To the* Murderer] Get thee gone;   30
    tomorrow
We 'll hear ourselves again.[29]

              [*Exit* Murderer

LADY MACBETH

        My royal lord,
You do not give the cheer:[30] the feast is sold
That is not often vouched, while 't is a-making,
'T is given with welcome.[31] To feed were best at home.[32]   35
From thence,[33] the sauce to meat is ceremony;[34]
Meeting were bare without it.[35]

MACBETH

        Sweet remembrancer![36] –
Now, good digestion wait on[37] appetite,
And health on both!

38 *May it . . . sit?* – "Would you like to sit down, your highness?" But Macbeth does not notice the question, for he is thinking of Banquo.

39 *Here had we . . . Banquo present* – "We should now have had all the honourable people of our country (*our country's honour*) under this roof if only the gracious person of our Banquo had been present".

40 *Who may . . . unkindness* – "and I should more likely challenge him for (his) unkindness (at not coming to my feast)".

41 *To grace . . . royal company* – "give us the honour of your company as king (at the table)".

42 *The table 's full*, because the Ghost of Banquo is now sitting in Macbeth's place at the table. But only Macbeth himself can see it.

LENOX

May it please your highness sit?[38]

MACBETH

Here had we now our country's honour roofed,   40
Were the graced person of our Banquo present;[39]

The Ghost of BANQUO *enters, and*
sits in MACBETH'S *place.*

Who may I rather challenge for unkindness,[40]
Than pity for mischance!

ROSSE

His absence, Sir,
Lays blame upon his promise. Please 't your highness
To grace us with your royal company?[41]   45

MACBETH

The table 's full.[42]

LENOX

Here is a place reserved, Sir.

MACBETH

Where?

LENOX

Here, my good lord. [MACBETH *notices the* Ghost] What is 't
    that moves your highness?

MACBETH

Which of you have done this?

43 *it*, the murder. Macbeth hired other men to do it instead.

44 *upon a thought* – "in a moment". Lady Macbeth realises very quickly what is happening, and makes excuses for her husband.

45 *If much you note him* – "If you take a lot of notice of him".

46 *Are you a man?* – "Do you call yourself a man (and yet fear things which no one else can see)?"

47 *O proper stuff!* – "Rubbish!"

48 *the very painting of your fear* – "nothing but what your fear has pictured to you". Lady Macbeth goes on to compare this ghost with the vision of the dagger, which her husband must have told her about (II.i.33 ff.).

49 *air-drawn* – "pictured in the air".

50 *flaws* are sudden short storms, here storms of passion in Macbeth's behaviour.

51 *Impostors to true fear* – "false characters in comparison with true fear", because frightened by unworthy objects.

52 *Authorised by her grandam* – "first told by her grandmother".

53 *When all's done* – "As a matter of fact".

54 *You look but on a stool* – "you are only looking at a stool" (see illustration).

122

LORDS

What, my good lord?

MACBETH

[*To the* Ghost] Thou canst not say I did it.[43] Never shake   50
Thy gory locks at me.

ROSSE

Gentlemen, rise; his highness is not well.

LADY MACBETH

Sit, worthy friends. My lord is often thus,
And hath been from his youth: pray you, keep seat;
The fit is momentary; upon a thought[44]   55
He will again be well. If much you note him[45]
You shall offend him, and extend his passion;
Feed, and regard him not. – [*To* MACBETH] Are you a man?[46]

MACBETH

Ay, and a bold one, that dare look on that
Which might appal the devil.

LADY MACBETH

             O proper stuff![47]   60
This is the very painting of your fear:[48]
This is the air-drawn[49] dagger which, you said,
Led you to Duncan. O! these flaws[50] and starts
(Impostors to true fear[51]) would well become
A woman's story at a winter's fire,   65
Authorised by her grandam.[52] Shame itself!
Why do you make such faces? When all 's done,[53]
You look but on a stool.[54]

123

55 *charnel-houses* – "places where dead
bodies are laid".
56 *our monuments . . . of kites* – "our
monuments must be the stomachs
(*maws*) of kites", i.e. our bodies
will have to be given to birds of
prey to be eaten up if our graves
cannot hold them.
57 *folly* – "stupidity".
58 *i' th' olden time* – "in time past; in
history".
59 *Ere humane . . . weal* – "before
human (*humane*) statutes purified
the state (*weal*), making it gentle".
In history, before there were laws
to govern man's actions in the
state, and life was rougher, murders had been done.

60 *and since too* – "and since that time,
too".
61 *the time has been That* – "there was
a time when".
62 *twenty mortal murders on their
crowns*. Each of the *mortal murders*
is a wound which in itself could
kill a man. And, as the murderer
told Macbeth in line 27, Banquo
has twenty of these on his head.
63 *do lack you* – "miss your company".

MACBETH

[*To the* Lords] Pr'ythee, see there! behold! look! lo! how say
   you?
Why, what care I? [*To the* Ghost] If thou canst nod, speak too. –   70
[*To the* Lords] If charnel-houses[55] and our graves must send
Those that we bury back, our monuments
Shall be the maws of kites.[56]

                     [Ghost *disappears*

LADY MACBETH
        What! quite unmanned in folly?[57]

MACBETH

If I stand here, I saw him.

LADY MACBETH
        Fie! for shame!

MACBETH

Blood hath been shed ere now, i' th' olden time,[58]   75
Ere humane statute purged the gentle weal;[59]
Ay, and since too,[60] murders have been performed
Too terrible for the ear: the time has been
That,[61] when the brains were out, the man would die,
And there an end; but now they rise again,   80
With twenty mortal murders on their crowns,[62]
And push us from our stools. This is more strange
Than such a murder is.

LADY MACBETH
        My worthy lord,
Your noble friends do lack you.[63]

64 *muse* – "wonder".

65 *a strange infirmity.* He takes up his wife's explanation of the fit (lines 53–4).

66 *we thirst* – "we drink".

67 *all to all* – "all (good wishes) to all (of you)".

68 *Avaunt!* – "Go away!"

69 *speculation* – "understanding".

70 *man*, any man; Macbeth dares to do what any man will, but no man can fight against a spirit.

71 *Approach thou* – "Approach!" The sense also contains an idea of the condition: "If you approach . . ."

72 *armed* – "having armour"; the skin of a rhinoceros is very hard (see illustration).

73 *Hyrcan* – "Hyrcanian". Hyrcania was a district of the ancient empire of Persia; its tigers are mentioned in Pliny's *Natural History*.

74 *that*, i.e. that of a ghost.

The armed [72] *rhinoceros*

MACBETH

[*To* LADY MACBETH] I do forget. –
[*To the* Lords] Do not muse[64] at me, my most worthy friends;   85
I have a strange infirmity,[65] which is nothing
To those that know me. Come, love and health to all;
Then, I'll sit down. – Give me some wine: fill full: –
I drink to the general joy of the whole table,
And to our dear friend Banquo, whom we miss;   90
Would he were here.

Re-enter Ghost

To all, and him, we thirst,[66]
And all to all.[67]

LORDS

Our duties, and the pledge.

MACBETH

[*To the* Ghost] Avaunt![68] and quit my sight! let the earth
  hide thee!
Thy bones are marrowless, thy blood is cold;
Thou hast no speculation[69] in those eyes,   95
Which thou dost glare with.

LADY MACBETH

[*To the* Lords] Think of this, good peers,
But as a thing of custom: 't is no other;
Only it spoils the pleasure of the time.

MACBETH

What man[70] dare, I dare:
Approach thou[71] like the rugged Russian bear,   100
The armed[72] rhinoceros, or the Hyrcan[73] tiger;
Take any shape but that,[74] and my firm nerves

127

75 *dare me to the desert* – "challenge me (to fight) in some lonely place".

76 *If trembling . . . of a girl.* It is generally agreed that this passage is faulty, and should begin: *If, trembling, I inhibit thee . . .* – "If through fear (*trembling*) I (by using my royal authority), restrain you (from challenging me), declare me to have been the baby of a girl".

77 *being gone* – "(the ghost) having gone".

78 *broke* – "broken up, spoilt".

79 *admired* – "strange".

80 *overcome us* – "pass over us".

81 *special wonder* – "particular surprise".

82 *You make me . . . that I owe* – "You make me a stranger even to the character (*disposition*) which is my own." The general sense of the passage from line .110 is as follows: "Do you think that people can see ghosts and not be surprised? I cannot; but when I see that you are not frightened, you make me have doubts even about my own character."

83 *blanched with fear* – "made white with fear".

84 *Stand not . . . your going* – "Do not trouble to keep to the proper social order as you leave."

128

Shall never tremble: or, be alive again,
And dare me to the desert[75] with thy sword;
If trembling I inhabit then, protest me   105
The baby of a girl.[76] Hence, horrible shadow!
Unreal mockery, hence! –

[Ghost *disappears*

                Why, so; – being gone,[77]
I am a man again. – Pray you, sit still.

LADY MACBETH

[*To* MACBETH] You have displaced the mirth, broke[78] the good
   meeting,
With most admired[79] disorder.

MACBETH

               Can such things be,   110
And overcome us[80] like a summer's cloud,
Without our special wonder?[81] You make me strange
Even to the disposition that I owe,[82]
When now I think you can behold such sights,
And keep the natural ruby of your cheeks,   115
When mine is blanched with fear.[83]

ROSSE

             What sights, my lord?

LADY MACBETH

[*To the* Lords] I pray you, speak not; he grows worse and
   worse;
Question enrages him. At once, good night: –
Stand not upon the order of your going,[84]
But go at once.

85 *It will have blood, they say* – "People say that bloody deeds must have blood in return."

86 *Augurs.* An augur is a man learned in *auguries.* But here the word probably refers to the thing, not the person: *augury* – "sign in nature, especially connected with the flight of birds, believed to show what would happen in the future."

87 *understood relations* – "relations (between cause and effect) when understood (by those who study supernatural signs)".

88 *magot-pies* – "magpies".

89 *choughs* – "crows".

90 *brought forth . . . of blood* – "revealed the most carefully hidden (*secret'st*) murderer".

91 *What is the night?* – "What time of night is it?"

92 *at odds* – "in disagreement"; the night and the morning are in disagreement as to which is which, whether it is, in fact, night or morning.

93 *How say'st . . . great bidding* – "What do you think about Macduff, who refuses to present himself at my strong command?"

94 *I hear it by the way* – "Someone has told me in conversation"; Macbeth did not actually send for him.

95 *them,* i.e. the lords whom Macbeth suspects.

96 *fee'd* – "employed", as a secret informer.

97 *betimes* – "early".

98 *bent* – "determined".

99 *For mine own . . . way* – "compared with my own good, all other considerations must take second place".

130

LENOX

Good night, and better health   120
Attend his majesty!

LADY MACBETH

A kind good night to all.

[*Exeunt* Lords *and* Attendants

MACBETH

It will have blood, they say,[85] blood will have blood:
Stones have been known to move, and trees to speak;
Augurs,[86] and understood relations,[87] have
By magot-pies[88] and choughs,[89] and rooks, brought forth   125
The secret'st man of blood.[90] What is the night?[91]

LADY MACBETH

Almost at odds[92] with morning, which is which.

MACBETH

How say'st thou, that Macduff denies his person
At our great bidding?[93]

LADY MACBETH

Did you send to him, Sir?

MACBETH

I hear it by the way;[94] but I will send.   130
There 's not a one of them,[95] but in his house
I keep a servant fee'd.[96] I will tomorrow
(And betimes[97] I will) to the weird sisters:
More shall they speak; for now I am bent[98] to know,
By the worst means, the worst. For mine own good   135
All causes shall give way:[99] I am in blood
Stepped in so far, that, should I wade no more,

131

100 *should I wade . . . as go o'er* – "even if I waded no more (through the river of blood), it would be as difficult to go back as to go over to the other side".

101 *in head* – "in my mind". In this line *head* and *hand* (i.e. thought and action) are to be taken together.

102 *that will to hand* – "that must be put into action".

103 *Which must . . . scanned* – "which must be done before they are thought about (*scanned*)".

104 *season* – "seasoning, preservative that keeps things fresh".

105 *natures* – "lives".

106 *My strange . . . hard use* – "My strange self-deception is the fear of a beginner (*the initiate fear*); it needs the experience that hardens one".

107 *young* – "inexperienced".

1 *Hecate* has been mentioned before as the goddess of witchcraft (e.g. III.ii.41).

2 *how now?* – "what (is the matter) now?"

3 *beldams* – "old women".

4 *trade and traffic* – "have dealings".

5 *close* – "secret".

6 *a wayward son* – "a man who is childish and self-willed", i.e. Macbeth, even though the description does not seem to suit him very well.

7 *Loves for . . . for you* – "likes to use your arts for his own purposes, not because he likes you yourselves".

8 *the pit of Acheron* – the deep place of the river Acheron, said to be a river of the lower world haunted by spirits of the dead.

Returning were as tedious as go o'er.[100]
Strange things I have in head,[101] that will to hand,[102]
Which must be acted, ere they may be scanned.[103]   140

LADY MACBETH

You lack the season[104] of all natures,[105] sleep.

MACBETH

Come, we 'll to sleep. My strange and self-abuse
Is the initiate fear, that wants hard use:[106]
We are yet but young[107] in deed.

[*Exeunt*

Scene V. The heath.

Thunder. Enter the THREE WITCHES, *meeting* HECATE.[1]

I WITCH

Why, how now,[2] Hecate? you look angerly.

HECATE

Have I not reason, beldams[3] as you are,
Saucy, and overbold? How did you dare
To trade and traffic[4] with Macbeth,
In riddles, and affairs of death;   5
And I, the mistress of your charms,
The close[5] contriver of all harms,
Was never called to bear my part,
Or show the glory of our art?
And, which is worse, all you have done   10
Hath been but for a wayward son,[6]
Spiteful and wrathful; who, as others do,
Loves for his own ends, not for you.[7]
But make amends now: get you gone,
And at the pit of Acheron[8]   15

133

9 *wrought* – "done".

10 *sleights* – "tricks".

11 *and bear . . . grace and fear* – "and remain hopeful in spite of (the warnings of) wisdom, honour and fear".

12 *security* – "a feeling of safety where there is no cause to feel safe; false security".

13 *stays* – "waits". Important spirits such as Hecate were said to have attendant spirits to wait on them. Hecate is called by her attendant spirit with the song "*Come away, come away*".

This scene is generally considered not to have been written by Shakespeare. It adds almost nothing to the story of the play, which is otherwise fast-moving; some of the statements do not seem to be in character; and it is out of place to declare that Macbeth is now to be drawn on *to his confusion* because he has displeased the witches and their mistress.

Meet me i' the morning: thither he
Will come to know his destiny.
Your vessels and your spells provide,
Your charms, and everything beside.
I am for the air; this night I 'll spend   20
Unto a dismal and a fatal end:
Great business must be wrought[9] ere noon.
Upon the corner of the moon
There hangs a vaporous drop profound;
I 'll catch it ere it come to ground: 25
And that, distilled by magic sleights,[10]
Shall raise such artificial sprites,
As, by the strength of their illusion,
Shall draw him on to his confusion.
He shall spurn fate, scorn death, and bear   30
His hopes 'bove wisdom, grace and fear;[11]
And you all know, security[12]
Is mortals' chiefest enemy.

       [*Song, within*: "Come away, come away," etc.

Hark! I am called: my little spirit, see,
Sits in a foggy cloud, and stays[13] for me.   35

                                      [*Exit*

I WITCH

Come, let 's make haste: she 'll soon be back again.

                                      [*Exeunt*

(III.vi) Lenox tells another lord how his suspicions are now fairly roused against Macbeth. The lord tells him in return that Malcolm (as the rightful heir of Duncan) and Macduff have gone to England to raise forces against Macbeth.

1 *My former speeches* – "What I have already said". Lenox and the other lord have already been talking about recent events.

2 *have but hit your thoughts* – "have only given you the idea".

3 *Which can interpret farther* – "which (i.e. *your thoughts*) can themselves think out things more deeply".

4 *Things have been strangely borne* – "things have happened very strangely".

5 *of Macbeth* – "by Macbeth".

6 *marry* was a common exclamation. (See II.iii.24 and the note to it.)

7 *walked too late* – "was out of doors too late at night", so late that he was killed.

8 *Who cannot want the thought* – "Is there anybody who cannot think".

9 *fact* – "deed; what is done".

10 *straight* – "at once".

11 *the two delinquents tear* – "tear (to pieces) the two delinquents"; the chamberlains were delinquents because they should have been looking after Duncan, the king, while he was asleep.

12 *any heart alive* – "any thinking and feeling person".

13 *deny 't* – "say that they were not responsible (for the murder of the king)".

14 *He has borne all things well* – "he has managed everything well".

15 *under his key* – "in his keeping".

16 *an 't* – "if it".

17 *What 't were to kill a father* – "what it means to kill a father". Lenox thinks that Macbeth would kill them and pretend that he was punishing them for the murder of their father.

18 *for from broad words* (line 21) . . . *in disgrace* – "for I hear Macduff lives in disgrace because of his plain speaking (*from broad words*) and because he did not present himself (*failed His presence*) at the tyrant's feast". Macbeth asked after him (III.iv.128 ff.) but apparently did not actually invite him.

19 *can you tell* – "do you know".

20 *Where he bestows himself?* – "where he is staying".

21 *From whom . . . birth* – "from whom this tyrant holds back (*holds*) what is his birthright (*the due of birth*, kingship)".

22 *received Of* – "received (as a guest) by".

23 *the most pious Edward*. This is Edward, king of England, who was called "the Confessor" because he was *most pious*.

Scene VI. Somewhere in Scotland.

Enter LENOX *and another* Lord.

LENOX

My former speeches[1] have but hit your thoughts,[2]
Which can interpret farther:[3] only, I say,
Things have been strangely borne.[4] The gracious Duncan
Was pitied of Macbeth:[5] — marry,[6] he was dead; —
And the right-valiant Banquo walked too late;[7]   5
Whom, you may say, if 't please you, Fleance killed,
For Fleance fled. Men must not walk too late.
Who cannot want the thought[8] how monstrous
It was for Malcolm and for Donalbain
To kill their gracious father? damnèd fact![9]   10
How it did grieve Macbeth! did he not straight,[10]
In pious rage, the two delinquents tear,[11]
That were the slaves of drink, and thralls of sleep?
Was not that nobly done? Ay, and wisely, too;
For 't would have angered any heart alive[12]   15
To hear the men deny 't.[13] So that, I say,
He has borne all things well;[14] and I do think
That, had he Duncan's sons under his key[15]
(As, an 't[16] please Heaven, he shall not), they should find
What 't were to kill a father;[17] so should Fleance.   20
But, peace! — for from broad words, and 'cause he failed
His presence at the tyrant's feast, I hear
Macduff lives in disgrace.[18] Sir, can you tell[19]
Where he bestows himself?[20]

LORD

                    The son of Duncan,
From whom this tyrant holds the due of birth,[21]   25
Lives in the English court; and is received
Of[22] the most pious Edward[23] with such grace,
That the malevolence of fortune nothing

24 *the malevolence . . . high respect* – "the ill-will of fortune (against him) in no way reduces the high respect paid to him".

25 *upon his aid* – "in his (Macduff's) aid; to help him".

26 *To wake Northumberland* – "stir into action the Earl of Northumberland (against the Scottish tyrant)".

27 *That* – "to the end that".

28 *Him above* – "God in Heaven".

29 *Free from . . . bloody knives* – "free our feasts and banquets from the knives of murderers".

30 *Do faithful homage* – "pay honour and respect to our rightful lords". The lord looks back to the time when each man had a lord, and each lord an overlord, and all were eventually responsible to the king. At its best, this form of government, known as the feudal system, brought peace and security. With Macbeth on the throne many felt they had no overlord, for he was not their rightful king.

31 *receive free honours* – "receive those honours which are the right of free men".

32 *exasperate* for *exasperated* – "greatly angered".

33 *Sent he to Macduff?* – "Did he send (a messenger) to Macduff?"

34 *with an absolute* "*Sir, not I*" – "with (as an answer from Macduff to the invitation) a flat 'Sir, not I' ('Sir, tell him that *I* shall not come')".

35 *cloudy* – "disagreeable".

36 *turns me his back* – "turns his back on him; turns to go".

37 *hums*, as a sign of bad temper.

38 *as who should say* – "like someone who would say".

39 "*You 'll rue . . . this answer*" – "You'll be sorry for (*rue*) the time you hindered me with this answer." The messenger will be slow in returning to his master because the message he carries is an unpleasant one.

40 *And that well . . . a caution* – "And that (the messenger's behaviour) might well advise him to be careful".

41 *to hold* – "to keep". He would be well advised to keep as far away from Macbeth as possible – "to keep his distance", as we should now say.

42 *unfold* – "reveal".

43 *a hand accursed* – "a hated ruler".

Takes from his high respect.[24] Thither Macduff
Is gone to pray the holy king, upon his aid,[25]   30
To wake Northumberland,[26] and warlike Siward;
That,[27] by the help of these (with Him above[28]
To ratify the work), we may again
Give to our tables meat, sleep to our nights,
Free from our feasts and banquets bloody knives,[29]   35
Do faithful homage,[30] and receive free honours,[31]
All which we pine for now. And this report
Hath so exasperate[32] the king that he
Prepares for some attempt of war.

LENOX

Sent he to Macduff?[33]

LORD

He did: and with an absolute "Sir, not I,"[34]   40
The cloudy[35] messenger turns me his back,[36]
And hums,[37] as who should say,[38] "You 'll rue the time
That clogs me with this answer."[39]

LENOX

                    And that well might
Advise him to a caution,[40] to hold[41] what distance
His wisdom can provide. Some holy angel   45
Fly to the court of England, and unfold[42]
His message ere he come, that a swift blessing
May soon return to this our suffering country
Under a hand accursed![43]

LORD

I 'll send my prayers with him.

                                                    [Exeunt

139

(IV.i) The three witches are chanting and telling what they use for their spells when Macbeth comes to consult them again. Apparitions are called up by the witches in answer to his need for knowing about the future. The first, an armed head, warns him against Macduff; he wants to know more about this, but the spirit will not obey his orders. The second, a child covered in blood, says he need fear "none of woman born". The third, a child, with a tree in its hand, says that Macbeth will not be defeated until the word of Birnam moves to the hill of Dunsinane. Macbeth is still not satisfied; he wants to know whether in fact Banquo's children, and not his own, will be kings in the future. There is a display of eight kings, the last carrying a mirror which reflects many more; and the ghost of Banquo follows them. These stand for the future kings of Scotland, and are the heirs of Banquo.

As the witches disappear, Macbeth calls to Lenox, who has been waiting at a distance. Lenox tells him that Macduff has gone to England, and Macbeth, vowing that from now on he will not pause to consider taking action, determines to kill the family which Macduff has left behind him in Scotland.

1 *a boiling cauldron*. This cauldron is a pot into which the weird sisters put many things to work their charms. They dance round the pot singing as they go, and so Macbeth finds them when he comes to them to learn more of the future.

2 *the brinded cat; brinded* – "lined with different colours". Each witch has a "familiar spirit", which waits on her and does what she tells it. The first witch has a cat, the second a hedgehog (*hedge-pig*), and the third a spirit called Harpier.

3 *Harpier* is probably a form of *harpy*, a monster half woman and half bird.

4 *cries* – "calls out" (see illustration p. 142).

5 *'t is time*, time to begin working the charms.

6 *Round about the cauldron go*. The witches' lines from now on have a steady beat of four heavy syllables, reflecting the movement of the dancing round the cauldron.

7 *cold stone*. Many editors change this to *coldest stone*, so that the regular pattern of the lines is not broken. But the voice may stop on *cold* for the length of two syllables:
Toad, that under cold – stone.

8 *Days and nights . . . sleeping got* – "(toad that) has sweated poison (*Sweltered venom*), produced while it was asleep (*sleeping got*), for thirty-one days and nights".

9 *th' charmèd pot*. The second syllable of *charmèd* is pronounced and *i' th'* run into one:
Boil thou first i' th' charmèd pot

10 *Double, double, toil and trouble* – "Toil and trouble, double yourselves; make yourselves twice what you were!"

11 *fenny* – "belonging to the mud".

12 *Adder's fork* – "the forked tongue of the adder".

13 *howlet's* – "little owl's".

ACT FOUR

Scene I. A dark cave.
In the middle, a boiling cauldron.[1]
Thunder. Enter the THREE WITCHES

I WITCH

Thrice the brinded cat[2] hath mewed.

2 WITCH

Thrice, and once the hedge-pig whined.

3 WITCH

Harpier[3] cries,[4] 't is time,[5] 't is time.

I WITCH

Round about the cauldron go;[6]
In the poisoned entrails throw. –
Toad, that under cold stone[7]   5
Days and nights has thirty-one
Sweltered venom, sleeping got,[8]
Boil thou first i' th' charmèd pot.[9]

ALL

Double, double, toil and trouble:[10]   10
Fire, burn; and cauldron, bubble.

2 WITCH

Fillet of a fenny[11] snake,
In the cauldron boil and bake;
Eye of newt, and toe of frog,
Wool of bat, and tongue of dog,   15
Adder's fork,[12] and blind-worm's sting,
Lizard's leg, and howlet's[13] wing,

141

14 *a hell-broth* – "a strong, thick soup for the devil".

15 *Witches' mummy* – "medicine prepared by witches with powder made from a mummy".

16 *maw* – "stomach".

17 *gulf* – "what swallows up; stomach".

18 *ravined* – "full of prey".

19 *digged* for *dug* (up). Hemlock gives a poison.

20 *blaspheming*, because not Christian.

21 *slips of yew* – "thin shavings taken from a yew tree". These were thought to be poisonous, and certainly are to animals. And since the yew can often be seen growing in English churchyards, it has a certain mystery about it.

22 *Slivered* – "stripped off".

23 *the moon's eclipse*. An eclipse of the moon was thought to be a most unlucky sign, and therefore well suited to evil plans.

24 *birth-strangled babe* – "baby killed by stopping its breath at birth".

25 *Ditch-delivered by a drab* – "born to a bad woman in a ditch".

26 *slab* – "sticky".

27 *chaudron* – "stomach".

28 *I commend your pains* – "I praise your efforts".

29 *every one* – "each one of you".

Harpier³

1 WITCH

Speak.

2 WITCH

Demand.

3 WITCH

We 'll answer.

1 WITCH

Say, if thou 'dst[47] rather hear it from our mouths,
Or from our masters.

MACBETH

Call 'em; let me see 'em.

1 WITCH

Pour in sow's blood, that[48] hath eaten
Her nine farrow,[49] grease, that 's sweaten[50]   65
From the murderer's gibbet, throw
Into the flame.

ALL

Come, high or low,[51]
Thyself, and office, deftly show.[52]

Thunder. First Apparition, *an armed head.*[53]

MACBETH

Tell me, thou unknown power, –

1 WITCH

He knows thy thought:
Hear his speech, but say thou nought.   70

147

54 *Descends.* Spirits and apparitions in the theatre appeared and disappeared through a trap-door in the floor of the stage.

55 *harped* – "guessed".

56 *a bloody child* – "a child covered in blood". This vision probably stands for Macduff at birth (see v.viii.15–16). In the end, Macduff (the bloody child) is *more potent* (line 76) than Macbeth, whose head came as the first apparition.

57 *none of woman born* – "nobody born of woman".

58 *of thee* – "from you".

59 *I'll make assurance . . . bond of fate* – "I'll make what is already certain doubly certain by taking out a binding agreement with fate."

60 *That I may tell . . . it lies* – "(I'll kill you) so that I shall be able to say to pale-hearted Fear, 'You are a liar' (because there will then be no need for fear to exist)".

61 *sleep in spite of thunder,* i.e. sleep through the troubled times (*thunder*) without feeling frightened.

the murderer's gibbet

I APPARITION

Macbeth! Macbeth! Macbeth! beware Macduff;
Beware the Thane of Fife. – Dismiss me. – Enough.

[*Descends*[54]

MACBETH

Whate'er thou art, for thy good caution, thanks:
Thou hast harped[55] my fear aright. But one word more: –

I WITCH

He will not be commanded. Here 's another,   75
More potent than the first.

.   *Thunder. Second* Apparition, *a bloody child.*[56]

2 APPARITION

Macbeth! Macbeth! Macbeth! –

MACBETH

Had I three ears, I 'd hear thee.

2 APPARITION

Be bloody, bold and resolute: laugh to scorn
The power of man, for none of woman born[57]   80
Shall harm Macbeth.

[*Descends*

MACBETH

Then live, Macduff: what need I fear of thee?[58]
But yet I 'll make assurance double sure,
And take a bond of fate:[59] thou shalt not live;
That I may tell pale-hearted Fear it lies.[60]   85
And sleep in spite of thunder.[61] –

62 *issue* – "child".
63 *the round And top of sovereignty* – "the crown (as a sign) of kingship".
64 *lion-mettled* – "as brave as a lion".
65 *Who chafes* – "who annoys (you)".
66 *frets* – "worries (you)".
67 *Great Birnam wood . . . high Dunsinane hill.* Birnam and Dunsinane are places near Perth in Scotland, lying about 20 kilometres apart. Birnam is a hill-top covered with trees; at Dunsinane there was a defence post owned by Macbeth.

68 *impress the forest* – "force the forest to do military service".
69 *Sweet bodements!* – "Happy things foretold!"
70 *the lease of nature* – "the length of time of natural life: *lease* suggests an agreement to live somewhere for a certain time; and this, he continues, must be paid for, with his breath.
71 *mortal custom* – "natural death". The breath is "paid" to time and natural death for the "lease of life"; but the lease comes to an end at last.

Thunder. Third Apparition, *a child*
crowned, with a tree in his hand.

What is this,
That rises like the issue[62] of a king;
And wears upon his baby brow the round
And top of sovereignty?[63]

ALL

Listen, but speak not to 't.

3 APPARITION

Be lion-mettled,[64] proud, and take no care   90
Who chafes,[65] who frets,[66] or where conspirers are:
Macbeth shall never vanquished be, until
Great Birnam wood to high Dunsinane hill[67]
Shall come against him.

[*Descends*

MACBETH

That will never be:
Who can impress the forest;[68] bid the tree   95
Unfix his earth-bound root? Sweet bodements![69] good!
Rebellious dead, rise never, till the wood
Of Birnam rise; and our high-placed Macbeth
Shall live the lease of nature,[70] pay his breath
To time and mortal custom.[71] – Yet my heart   100
Throbs to know one thing: tell me (if your art
Can tell so much), shall Banquo's issue ever
Reign in this kingdom?

ALL

Seek to know no more.

151

72 *I will be satisfied* – "I insist on being satisfied (with an answer)".

73 *A show of eight Kings* is brought up in answer to Macbeth's question about Banquo (lines 102–3 above). He recognises the spirit of Banquo following them, and sees the last king holding a mirror; in the mirror the line is reflected, making a longer line still. This suggests that the descendants of Banquo will stretch out into the future as kings, and Banquo is, in fact, looked upon as a forerunner of the royal house of Stuart; it was James Stuart, King James VI of Scotland, who became King James I of England, and who was on the throne when *Macbeth* was written.

74 *Thy crown does sear mine eye-balls* – "your crown burns my eyes", because it is bright, and is also the sign of kingship, the prize which Macbeth himself fears to lose.

75 *Thou other gold-bound brow* – "you second brow with a gold crown on".

76 *to th' crack of doom* – "to the end of the world". (*Doom* or *doomsday* is the day of judgement after death.)

MACBETH

I will be satisfied:⁷² deny me this,
And an eternal curse fall on you! let me know. –   105
Why sinks that cauldron? and what noise is this?

[*Hautboys*

1 WITCH

Show!

2 WITCH

Show!

3 WITCH

Show!

ALL

Show his eyes, and grieve his heart;   110
Come like shadows, so depart.

*A show of eight Kings,*⁷³ *the last with a
glass in his hand*: BANQUO's Ghost *following.*

MACBETH

[*To the first King in the show*] Thou art too like the spirit of
   Banquo: down!
Thy crown does sear mine eye-balls:⁷⁴ [*To the second King*] and
   thy hair,
Thou other gold-bound brow,⁷⁵ is like the first: –
[*To the* WITCHES] A third is like the former: – filthy hags!   115
Why do you show me this? – a fourth? – Start, eyes!
What! will the line stretch out to th' crack of doom.⁷⁶
Another yet? – A seventh? – I 'll see no more: –
And yet the eighth appears, who bears a glass
Which shows me many more; and some I see   120

153

77 *two-fold balls.* The ball here is the golden ball, called an orb, which a king holds in his hand when he is crowned; it is a sign of his power on earth. The kings who hold *two-fold* balls are those who will rule over two kingdoms, Scotland and England.

78 *treble sceptres*; the three sceptres probably stand for England, Scotland and Ireland. (See glossary for *sceptre*.)

79 *the blood-boltered Banquo* – "Banquo, with his hair matted in dry blood".

80 *points at them for his* – "points at them as his (own descendants)".

81 *amazèdly* – "confusedly".

82 *antic round* – "curious dance".

83 *aye* – "forever".

84 *without there* – "(you who are) outside there".

154

That two-fold balls[77] and treble sceptres[78] carry.
Horrible sight! – Now, I see 't is true;
For the blood-boltered Banquo[79] smiles upon me,
And points at them for his.[80] – What! is this so?

I WITCH

Ay, Sir, all this is so: – but why   125
Stands Macbeth thus amazèdly?[81]
Come, sisters, cheer we up his sprites,
And show the best of our delights.
I'll charm the air to give a sound,
While you perform your antic round;[82]   130
That this great king may kindly say,
Our duties did his welcome pay.

[*Music. The* WITCHES *dance, and vanish with* HECATE

MACBETH

Where are they? Gone? – Let this pernicious hour
Stand aye[83] accursèd in the calendar! –
Come in, without there![84]

Enter LENOX

LENOX

What 's your grace's will?   135

MACBETH

Saw you the weird sisters?

LENOX

No, my lord.

MACBETH

Came they not by you?

155

85 *the air whereon they ride*. It was said that witches could ride through the air (e.g. on broomsticks).

86 *horse* – "a company of horse; horses".

87 *thou anticipat'st my dread exploits* – "you prevent my frightful acts" (by allowing something to happen – here the flight of Macduff to England – which takes away the opportunity of carrying them out).

88 *The flighty purpose . . . go with it* – "the quickly-passing aim (*flighty purpose*) is never overtaken (*o'ertook*) unless the deed goes with it". Unless the plan is laid and the deed done at the same time, the deed never catches up with the plan. Macbeth had thought of the murder of Macduff; but as he did not carry it out at once, he lost the opportunity of doing it at all.

89 *firstlings* – "first things"; in his heart they are ideas, in his hand actions.

90 *surprise* – "attack by surprise".

91 *give to th' edge o' th' sword* – "kill".

92 *That trace him in his line* – "that follow (*trace*) him in his line (of descent)".

93 *before this purpose cool* – "before this plan becomes cooler". Last time he made the mistake of thinking at once but delaying the action.

LENOX

No, indeed, my lord.

MACBETH

Infected be the air whereon they ride;[85]
And damned all those that trust them! – I did hear
The galloping of horse:[86] who was 't came by?   140

LENOX

'T is two or three, my lord, that bring you word,
Macduff is fled to England.

MACBETH

Fled to England?

LENOX

Ay, my good lord.

MACBETH

[*Aside*] Time, thou anticipat'st my dread exploits:[87]
The flighty purpose never is o'ertook,   145
Unless the deed go with it.[88] From this moment
The very firstlings[89] of my heart shall be
The firstlings of my hand. And even now,
To crown my thoughts with acts, be it thought and done:
The castle of Macduff I will surprise,[90]
Seize upon Fife; give to th' edge o' th' sword[91]   150
His wife, his babes, and all unfortunate souls
That trace him in his line.[92] No boasting, like a fool;
This deed I 'll do, before this purpose cool:[93]
But no more sights! – [*To* LENOX] Where are these gentlemen? 155
Come, bring me where they are.

[*Exeunt*

(IV.ii) In Macduff's castle in Fife, Rosse tries to convince Lady Macduff that her husband's flight to England was, after all, a good action. She remains unconvinced, and is frightened of what might happen to her and her family. Rosse is deeply touched and leaves her alone with her little son, who talks to her about his father. A messenger rushes in to say that their lives are in danger, but she and her family have nowhere to go for protection; murderers enter and kill them all.

1 *he*, i.e. Macduff.
2 *when our actions . . . us traitors* – "when our actions do not make us traitors, our fears do". When we are not traitors in anything that we do, our fears, which make us run away, show us to be traitors nevertheless.

3 *mansion* – "home".
4 *titles* – "property".
5 *himself* – "he himself".
6 *He wants the natural touch* – "he lacks the natural feelings of humanity".
7 *Her young ones in her nest.* This goes with *wren* in line 9: "the poor wren . . . with her young ones in her nest, will fight against the owl", even though she has no hope of winning.
8 *All is the fear . . . the love* – "(To him) the fear is everything; the love (of family) is nothing."
9 *As little is the wisdom* – "the wisdom is as small (as the love)".
10 *school yourself* – "teach yourself (to be patient and understanding in your sorrow)".
11 *The fits o' th' season* – "the sudden troubles of the present time (*season*)"; for *fits*, compare *life's fitful fever* (III.ii.23).

Scene II. Fife.
A room in MACDUFF'S *castle.*
Enter LADY MACDUFF, *her* Son, *and* ROSSE

LADY MACDUFF

What had he[1] done, to make him fly the land?

ROSSE

You must have patience, madam.

LADY MACDUFF

　　　　　　　　He had none:
His flight was madness: when our actions do not,
Our fears do make us traitors.[2]

ROSSE

　　　　　　　You know not
Whether it was his wisdom or his fear.　　　　　　5

LADY MACDUFF

Wisdom! to leave his wife, to leave his babes,
His mansion,[3] and his titles,[4] in a place
From whence himself[5] does fly? He loves us not:
He wants the natural touch;[6] for the poor wren,
The most diminutive of birds, will fight,　　　　　10
Her young ones in her nest,[7] against the owl.
All is the fear, and nothing is the love;[8]
As little is the wisdom,[9] where the flight
So runs against all reason.

ROSSE

　　　　　　　My dearest coz,
I pray you, school yourself:[10] but, for your husband,　　15
He is noble, wise, judicious, and best knows
The fits o' th' season.[11] I dare not speak much further:

12 *we are traitors . . . know ourselves* – "we are traitors, but do not know ourselves (to be so)", for whatever is done may be understood as unfaithfulness to one side or another.

13 *we hold rumour . . . what we fear.* Rosse is very much affected by Lady Macduff's hopeless situation, and his words become broken and go along in fits and starts, like the troubled times. Here he seems to mean: "we do not really know what we have to fear, because even the things we are frightened of are known only by rumour".

14 *move.* Rosse seems to break off his sentence here unfinished; he is thinking of some comparison between the troubled times and the movement of the sea, but it is not completed.

15 *Shall* for *It shall* (or possibly *I shall*). Again, Rosse is too moved to speak quite naturally or plainly.

16 *Things at the worst . . . were before* – "If things are as bad as they can be, they will either stop or get better."

17 *Blessing upon you!* – "God's blessing be upon you!'

18 *Fathered he is* – "He had a father".

19 *my disgrace* – "a disgrace to me". He is so moved by the scene that he fears he will cry.

20 *Sirrah* – "Little fellow".

21 *with* – "on".

22 *what* – "whatever".

But cruel are the times, when we are traitors,
And do not know ourselves;[12] when we hold rumour
From what we fear, yet know not what we fear,[13]   20
But float upon a wild and violent sea
Each way, and move[14] – I take my leave of you:
Shall[15] not be long but I 'll be here again.
Things at the worst will cease, or else climb upward
To what they were before.[16] – [*To her* Son] My, pretty
    cousin,   25
Blessing upon you![17]

LADY MACDUFF

Fathered he is,[18] and yet he 's fatherless.

ROSSE

I am so much a fool, should I stay longer,
It would be my disgrace[19] and your discomfort:
I take my leave at once.   30

                                                             [*Exit*

LADY MACDUFF

[*To her* Son] Sirrah,[20] your father 's dead:
And what will you do now? How will you live?

SON

As birds do, mother.

LADY MACDUFF

What, with[21] worms and flies?

SON

With what[22] I get, I mean; and so do they.

7—M.   161

23 *thou 'dst never fear* – "would you never be frightened of . . .?"

24 *the net . . . the gin.* These are various traps for catching birds; a *gin* (from *engine*) was a mechanical trap.

25 *Poor birds . . . set for* – "They (i.e. these traps) are not set for *poor* birds (but for rich ones)"; his mother has just called him *Poor bird* (line 35).

26 *for all your saying* – "in spite of everything you say".

27 *how wilt thou do for a father?* – "what will you do for a father – how will you manage without one?"

28 *I can buy . . . any market* – "I can get another one very easily"; she speaks as if she could buy one. Her son continues this light touch by saying (in the next line) that she would buy them to sell again, i.e. she would not take another husband at all.

29 *Thou speakest with . . . enough or thee; wit* here is probably used first to mean "cleverness in humorous conversation", and second "cleverness" alone. – "You speak with all the humour (*wit*) you have (by continuing my playful remark – but that is not enough); and yet, indeed (*i' faith*), it may be all the cleverness (*wit*) you need (in this situation)."

30 *Ay, that he was* – "Yes, he was that".

LADY MACDUFF

Poor bird! thou 'dst never fear[23] the net, nor lime,   35
The pit-fall, nor the gin?[24]

SON

        Why should I, mother?
Poor birds they are not set for.[25]
My father is not dead, for all your saying.[26]

LADY MACDUFF

Yes, he is dead: how wilt thou do for a father?[27]

SON

Nay, how will you do for a husband?   40

LADY MACDUFF

Why, I can buy me twenty at any market.[28]

SON

Then you 'll buy 'em to sell again.

LADY MACDUFF

Thou speakest with all thy wit;
And yet, i' faith, with wit enough for thee.[29]

SON

Was my father a traitor, mother?   45

LADY MACDUFF

Ay, that he was.[30]

SON

What is a traitor?

31 *one that swears and lies*, i.e. one who is false to his promises of allegiance. Macduff is a traitor to Macbeth because he has turned against his king, but Lady Macduff does not want to tell her son so. The son, however, takes it up, and again speaks with all his wit.

32 *be all traitors that do so?* – "are they all traitors who do this (swear and lie)?"

33 *Then the liars . . . hang up them: enow* – "enough"; *hang up them* – "hang them (up)". If the lying and swearing make them traitors, then there are so many traitors, he thinks, that they could all come together and beat the honest men.

34 *poor monkey* is used as a term of endearment for the child.

35 *if you would not . . . new father.* If Macduff is really dead, and his wife is not weeping for him, then it is a sure sign that she has another lover, whom she will quickly marry, and who will then become a new father to her son.

LADY MACDUFF

Why, one that swears and lies.[31]

SON

And be all traitors that do so?[32]

LADY MACDUFF

Every one that does so is a traitor, and must be hanged.   50

SON

And must they all be hanged that swear and lie?

LADY MACDUFF

Every one.

SON

Who must hang them?

LADY MACDUFF

Why, the honest men.

SON

Then the liars and swearers are fools; for there are liars and   55
swearers enow to beat the honest men, and hang up them.[33]

LADY MACDUFF

Now God help thee, poor monkey![34] But how wilt thou do
for a father?

SON

If he were dead, you 'ld weep for him: if you would not, it
were a good sign that I should quickly have a new father.[35]   60

36 *Though in . . . am perfect* – "though I know all about your social position" (she is the wife of a thane, and this messenger has rushed in to her, not waiting to be brought in by a servant).

37 *I doubt* – "I fear (that)".

38 *nearly*, i.e. "and is very near".

39 *homely* – "ordinary".

40 *hence* – "(go) away".

41 *To fright . . . too savage* – "I think I am too rough even to frighten you in this way".

42 *To do worse . . . your person* – "to do worse to you (than frighten you with my wild manner) would be (like the) inhuman (*fell*) cruelty which is too near to you (*nigh your person*)".

43 *Accounted* – "considered (to be)".

44 *in no place . . . may'st find him* – "in no place so unholy that a person of your sort (*such as thou*) might be there to find him".

LADY MACDUFF

Poor prattler, how thou talk'st!

Enter a Messenger

MESSENGER

Bless you, fair dame! I am not to you known,
Though in your state of honour I am perfect.[36]
I doubt,[37] some danger does approach you nearly:[38]
If you will take a homely[39] man's advice,   65
Be not found here; hence,[40] with your little ones.
To fright you thus, methinks, I am too savage;[41]
To do worse to you were fell cruelty,
Which is too nigh your person.[42] Heaven preserve you!
I dare abide no longer.

                                                      [*Exit*

to be praised

LADY MACDUFF

                    Whither should I fly?   70
I have done no harm. But I remember now
I am in this earthly world, where to do harm
Is often laudable, to do good sometime
Accounted[43] dangerous folly: why then, alas,
Do I put up that womanly defence,   75
To say, I have done no harm? What are these faces?

Enter Murderers

MURDERER

Where is your husband?

LADY MACDUFF

I hope, in no place so unsanctified,
Where such as thou may'st find him.[44]

45 *shag-eared* – "with long, rough hair over the ears".
46 *Young fry of treachery* – "Young child of a traitor".

(IV.iii) In England Macduff has found Malcolm and tries to stir him into action against Macbeth. To this Malcolm puts up unexpected difficulties: he professes to be immoral and miserly, and in every way unsuited to be a king. But this is only to test Macduff's loyalty, for Malcolm says that Macbeth has already sent him people who have tried to trick him into putting himself into the hands of Macbeth's agents. He is in fact in every way suited to be a king.

Rosse arrives with news of continued trouble in Scotland. Macduff asks about his wife and children, and Rosse has reluctantly to tell him that they are all dead. At first he is speechless, but quickly vows that nothing shall stand in the way between him and Macbeth.

1 *some desolate shade* – "some quiet sheltered place".
2 *bosoms* – "hearts".
3 *mortal* – "deadly".

MURDERER

He 's a traitor.

SON

Thou liest, thou shag-eared[45] villain!

MURDERER

What, you egg!   80

[*Stabbing him*

Young fry of treachery![46]

SON

He has killed me, mother:
Run away, I pray you!

[*Dies*

[*Exit* LADY MACDUFF, *crying "Murder!" and
pursued by the* Murderers.

Scene III. England.

A room in the King's palace.

Enter MALCOLM *and* MACDUFF.

MALCOLM

Let us seek out some desolate shade,[1] and there
Weep our sad bosoms[2] empty.

MACDUFF

Let us rather
Hold fast the mortal[3] sword, and like good men

4 *Bestride our down-fall birthdom* – "walk with the great steps (of a conqueror) over our fallen (*down-fall*) country (*birthdom*)".

5 *Each new morn* – "Every new morning."

6 *that* – "so that".

7 *Like syllable of dolour* – "similar cries of sorrow".

8 *What I believe, I 'll wail* – "I'll feel sorrow (only) for what I believe (to be true)"

9 *What know, believe* – "(I'll) believe (only) what I know."

10 *As I shall find the time to friend* – "whenever I find the time 'friendly', suitable".

11 *spoke* for *spoken.*

12 *perchance* – "perhaps".

13 *whose sole name* – "whose very name; whose name alone".

14 *deserve of him* – "get from him (for some service)".

15 *and wisdom* (line 15) . . . *an angry god.* Here Malcolm seems to suggest that Macduff (whom Macbeth has not, as far as they know, harmed in any way) should hand him (Malcolm) over to Macbeth as a traitor: "(it is) wisdom to offer a lamb (Malcolm) to make peace with an angry god (Macbeth)". This suggestion is not referred to again, but later (line 50 ff.) a different test of Macduff's loyalty is made.

16 *A good and virtuous . . . imperial charge* – "(Even) a good and honest character may give way (*recoil*) in the face of a royal (*imperial*) command."

17 *I shall crave your pardon* for making such a suggestion.

18 *That which . . . cannot transpose* – "my thoughts cannot make you different (*transpose*) from what you are".

19 *Angels are bright . . . brightest fell;* the brightest was Satan, who fell from the happiness of heaven because he was too proud. There are still loyal people even though some are disloyal.

20 *Though all things . . . look so* – "even though all wicked things want to have the look of grace, yet grace must still look what it is". It cannot change its looks just because other qualities try to look as it does.

21 *I have lost my hopes,* of successful opposition to Macbeth. As Malcolm has suggested that his loyalty is questionable, it would be unwise for Macduff to build up any hopes in him.

22 *Perchance even . . . my doubts; doubts* is taken as a contrast to *hopes* in the line before. Malcolm's doubts arise from Macduff's leaving his wife and children in Scotland and flying to England – as he goes on to explain.

23 *rawness* – "haste; lack of consideration".

170

Bestride our down-fall birthdom.[4] Each new morn,[5]
New widows howl, new orphans cry; new sorrows   5
Strike heaven on the face, that[6] it resounds
As if it felt with Scotland, and yelled out
Like syllable of dolour.[7]

MALCOLM

        What I believe, I 'll wail;[8]
What know, believe;[9] and what I can redress,
As I shall find the time to friend,[10] I will   10
What you have spoke,[11] it may be so, perchance.[12]
This tyrant, whose sole name[13] blisters our tongues,
Was once thought honest: you have loved him well;
He hath not touched you yet. I am young; but something
You may deserve of him[14] through me, and wisdom   15
To offer up a weak, poor, innocent lamb,
T' appease an angry god.[15]

MACDUFF

I am not treacherous.

MALCOLM

        But Macbeth is.
A good and virtuous nature may recoil
In an imperial charge.[16] But I shall crave your pardon:[17]   20
That which you are, my thoughts cannot transpose:[18]
Angels are bright still, though the brightest fell:[19]
Though all things foul would wear the brows of grace,
Yet grace must still look so.[20]

MACDUFF

        I have lost my hopes.[21]

MALCOLM

Perchance even there, where I did find my doubts.[22]   25
Why in that rawness[23] left you wife and child

24 *motives* – "causes of action".

25 *Let not my jealousies . . . safeties* – "Do not think of my suspicions as dishonour to yourself, but simply as measures for my own safety". But Macduff does not quite understand this, and turns away disappointed.

26 *Bleed, bleed,* from the wounds the country has suffered.

27 *Great tyranny* (line 32) . . . *is affeered!* – "Great tyranny (the rule of Macbeth in Scotland), lay your foundations (*basis*) down firmly (*sure*), because Goodness dare not stop you! Show the signs of your wickedness, for your title to them is made certain (*affeered*)."

28 *I would not be . . . tyrant's grasp.* Macduff is disappointed in Malcolm because of his suggestions that Macduff should come to terms with Macbeth. – "I would not be the villain you think me for the whole space that is in the tyrant's grasp (i.e. the land that Macbeth rules, Scotland)."

29 *the rich East* – "the rich countries of the East".

30 *to boot* – "in addition" (to the land of Scotland).

31 *in absolute fear of you* – "in real fear of you, of your loyalty". This is the end of the first test.

32 *sinks beneath the yoke.* The country is compared to an animal, made to draw a cart with a heavy yoke on its neck. When the weight is too much the animal falls. And the yoke has always been taken as a sign of oppression.

33 *withal* – "also".

34 *hands uplifted in my right* – "hands (of people in Scotland) lifted up, ready (to fight) for my right (to the throne)".

35 *gracious England* – "the gracious king of England".

36 *goodly thousands* – "good (in size), considerable numbers (of men)".

37 *for* – "in spite of".

38 *wear it* – "carry it".

39 *yet* – "nevertheless".

40 *vices* – "evils".

41 *More suffer* – "suffer more".

42 *and more* – "and in more".

43 *By* – "through".

44 *What should he be?* – "Who is he to be?"

(Those precious motives,[24] those strong knots of love)
Without leave-taking? – I pray you,
Let not my jealousies be your dishonours,
But mine own safeties:[25] you may be rightly just,   30
Whatever I shall think.

MACDUFF

                    Bleed, bleed,[26] poor country!
Great tyranny, lay thou thy basis sure,
For goodness dare not check thee! wear thou thy wrongs;
The title is affeered![27] – Fare thee well, lord:
I would not be the villain that thou thinkest   35
For the whole space that 's in the tyrant's grasp,[28]
And the rich East[29] to boot.[30]

MALCOLM

                    Be not offended:
I speak not as in absolute fear of you.[31]
I think our country sinks beneath the yoke;[32]
It weeps, it bleeds; and each new day a gash   40
Is added to her wounds: I think, withal,[33]
There would be hands uplifted in my right;[34]
And here, from gracious England,[35] have I offer
Of goodly thousands:[36] but, for [37] all this,
When I shall tread upon the tyrant's head,   45
Or wear it[38] on my sword, yet[39] my poor country
Shall have more vices[40] than it had before,
More suffer,[41] and more[42] sundry ways than ever,
By[43] him that shall succeed.

MACDUFF

                    What should he be?[44]

MALCOLM

It is myself, I mean; in whom I know   50

173

45 *particulars* – "particular kinds".

46 *opened* – "revealed".

47 *my confineless harms* – "my unlimited evil".

48 *legions* – "the ranks (of devils)".

49 *to top Macbeth* – "to exceed Macbeth (in evil)".

50 *I grant him bloody* – "I agree (with you) that he is bloodthirsty".

51 *Luxurious* – "full of evil desire".

52 *Sudden* – "hasty".

53 *smacking* – "tasting", i.e. with a touch of.

54 *there 's no bottom . . . voluptuousness* – "there is no limit (*bottom*) at all to my evil desires", in contrast to Macbeth's.

55 *matrons* – "mothers".

56 *and my desire* (line 63) . . . *my will* – "and my desire would overcome (*o'erbear*) all restraining checks (*continent impediments*) which stood in the way of my will".

57 *such an one* – "such a person (as I)".

58 *nature* – "life".

59 *been*, i.e. been the cause of.

60 *yet* – "nevertheless".

61 *Convey* – "arrange (in secret) for".

62 *the time you may so hoodwink* – "you can deceive (*hoodwink*) the world (*time*) in this way".

63 *That vulture in you; vulture* – "bird of prey", and hence "nature of such a bird, desire to seize on prey". There would be enough women dedicating themselves to Malcolm's service to satisfy all his desires.

174

All the particulars[45] of vice so grafted,
That, when they shall be opened,[46] black Macbeth
Will seem as pure as snow; and the poor state
Esteem him as a lamb, being compared
With my confineless harms.[47]

MACDUFF

             Not in the legions[48]   55
Of horrid hell can come a devil more damned
In evils, to top Macbeth.[49]

MALCOLM

             I grant him bloody,[50]
Luxurious,[51] avaricious, false, deceitful,
Sudden,[52] malicious, smacking[53] of every sin
That has a name; but there 's no bottom, none,   60
In my voluptuousness:[54] your wives, your daughters,
Your matrons[55] and your maids, could not fill up
The cistern of my lust; and my desire
All continent impediments would o'erbear,
That did oppose my will:[56] better Macbeth   65
Than such an one[57] to reign.

MACDUFF

             Boundless intemperance
In nature[58] is a tyranny; it hath been[59]
Th' untimely emptying of the happy throne,
And fall of many kings. But fear not yet[60]
To take upon you what is yours; you may   70
Convey[61] your pleasures in a spacious plenty,
And yet seem cold – the time you may so hoodwink:[62]
We have willing dames enough; there cannot be
That vulture in you,[63] to devour so many
As will to greatness dedicate themselves.   75
Finding it so inclined.

64 *With this* – "In addition to this".

65 *my most ill-composed affection* – "my exceedingly badly-formed character".

66 *staunchless* – "what cannot be stopped in its flow", hence "what cannot be satisfied".

67 *I should cut off . . . their lands* – "I would kill (*cut off*) the nobles (of Scotland) to get their lands from them."

68 *his jewels* – "the jewels of this man (for example)".

69 *and this other's house* – "and the house of that man (as another example)".

70 *more-having* – "having more", which will act like a sauce and make him more hungry than before.

71 *that* – "so that".

72 *forge Quarrels unjust* – "start quarrels without just cause".

73 *This avarice* (line 84) *. . . summer-seeming lust.* Macduff uses the image of a plant to speak of this avarice. The *lust* is *summer-seeming*, i.e. like summer, or suited to it, for it will not last through the winter of old age. But the avarice is "(like a plant which) grows more strongly and with a root which is more harmful (*pernicious*)."

74 *it hath been . . . slain kings* – "it (avarice) has been the sword (i.e. the cause of death) of (many of) our kings who were murdered".

75 *foisons* – "plentiful supplies".

76 *Of your mere own* – "belonging to you yourself". He is apparently referring to the *foisons* which will become Malcolm's when he is king of Scotland.

77 *All these are . . . weighed* – "All these things are bearable (*portable*) if they are balanced by (*weighed with*) virtues".

78 *the king-becoming graces* – "the virtues which are fitting for a king".

79 *stableness* – "stability, firmness".

80 *I have no relish of them* – "I have no trace of them in me." Compare the use of *relish* – "taste" with that of *smacking* in line 59 above.

81 *the division of each several crime* – "the various parts of each particular (*several*) crime".

82 *the sweet milk of concord;* milk is an image of peace and plenty, as a mother feeds her child in love and fulness.

83 *Uproar the universal peace* – "turn the order of the universe into uproar".

84 *confound All unity* – "destroy all unity", and so bring universal confusion.

MALCOLM

With this,[64] there grows
In my most ill-composed affection[65] such
A staunchless[66] avarice, that, were I king,
I should cut off the nobles for their lands;[67]
Desire his jewels,[68] and this other's house:[69]   80
And my more-having[70] would be as a sauce
To make me hunger more, that[71] I should forge
Quarrels unjust[72] against the good and loyal,
Destroying them for wealth.

MACDUFF

This avarice
Sticks deeper, grows with more pernicious root   85
Than summer-seeming lust;[73] and it hath been
The sword of our slain kings:[74] yet do not fear;
Scotland hath foisons[75] to fill up your will,
Of your mere own.[76] All these are portable,
With other graces weighed.[77]   90

MALCOLM

But I have none: the king-becoming graces,[78]
As justice, verity, temperance, stableness,[79]
Bounty, perseverance, mercy, lowliness,
Devotion, patience, courage, fortitude,
I have no relish of them;[80] but abound   95
In the division of each several crime,[81]
Acting it many ways. Nay, had I power, I should
Pour the sweet milk of concord[82] into hell,
Uproar the universal peace,[83] confound
All unity[84] on earth.

MACDUFF

O Scotland! Scotland!   100

177

85 *O nation miserable!* – "O miserable nation".

86 *an untitled tyrant, bloody-sceptered* – "a tyrant without a (true) title (to the throne), holding a sceptre (the sign of kingship) gained by blood".

87 *wholesome* – "good".

88 *By his own interdiction . . . his breed* – "by forbidding himself (to enter Scotland) stands accused, and curses his family (*breed*)" (a royal one), by being what he is.

89 *upon her knees*, i.e. in prayer.

90 *These evils . . . upon thyself* – "These evils you list as belonging to yourself."

91 *Hath* for "have".

92 *my breast* – "my heart".

93 *Child of integrity* – "born of, having its origin in integrity". So ends the second testing. Malcolm has pretended he is lustful and avaricious. He now shows why he thought it necessary to try Macduff's good faith by making this pretence.

94 *trains* – "tricks". Macbeth has tried to win Malcolm into his power by sending messengers with false declarations of love and friendship, and by many other tricks of this sort.

95 *modest wisdom . . . over-credulous haste* – "wisdom, in the form of modesty, pulls me back from over-hasty belief (in what people tell me)".

96 *God above . . . thee and me* – "(May) God in heaven control our relationship together."

97 *to* – "under".

98 *Unspeak . . . detraction* – "take back what I said against myself".

99 *taints and blames* – "faults and accusations".

100 *For strangers* – "as things (which are) foreign".

101 *never was forsworn* – "never swore falsely".

MALCOLM

If such a one be fit to govern, speak:
I am as I have spoken.

MACDUFF

Fit to govern?
No, not to live. – O nation miserable![85]
With an untitled tyrant, bloody-sceptered,[86]
When shalt thou see thy wholesome[87] days again,   105
Since that the truest issue of thy throne
By his own interdiction stands accused,
And does blaspheme his breed?[88] Thy royal father
Was a most sainted king: the queen that bore thee,
Oft'ner upon her knees[89] than on her feet,   110
Died every day she lived. Fare thee well!
These evils thou repeat'st upon thyself[90]
Hath[91] banished me from Scotland. – O my breast,[92]
Thy hope ends here!

MALCOLM

Macduff, this noble passion,
Child of integrity,[93] hath from my soul   115
Wiped the black scruples, reconciled my thoughts
To thy good truth and honour. Devilish Macbeth
By many of these trains[94] hath sought to win me
Into his power, and modest wisdom plucks me
From over-credulous haste:[95] but God above   120
Deal between thee and me![96] for even now
I put myself to[97] thy direction, and
Unspeak mine own detraction;[98] here abjure
The taints and blames[99] I laid upon myself
For strangers[100] to my nature. I am yet   125
Unknown to woman; never was forsworn;[101]
Scarcely have coveted what was mine own;
At no time broke my faith: would not betray
The devil to his fellow; and delight

179

102 *my first false . . . upon myself* –
"the first lie I have ever told was
this about myself".

103 *truly* – "in fact".

104 *Is thine . . . to command* – "is (ready)
to be commanded by you and my
poor country".

105 *Whither* – "and to that place" (the
poor country, Scotland).

106 *before thy here-approach* – "before
your coming here".

107 *Old Siward* is Earl of Northumberland and leader of the English
forces, and has gone off to Scotland to fight in the cause of the
rightful ruler.

108 *at a point* – "prepared".

109 *we 'll together* – "we'll go off
together".

110 *the chance of goodness . . . quarrel* –
"may the result (of our journey)
be as successful as our quarrel is
just".

111 *Enter a* Doctor. This Doctor speaks
of a strange power, believed in
Shakespeare's day to have been the
special gift of the kings and queens
of England. It was a royal "touch"
by which an illness called scrofula
or "the king's evil" could be
cured. The passage which follows
was perhaps put in to please the
king then reigning, James I.

112 *a crew* – "a crowd".

113 *wretched souls* – "poor people".

114 *That stay his cure* – "who are
waiting for his cure".

115 *their malady . . . assay of art* –
"their illness defeats the greatest
efforts of (medical) skill".

116 *Such sanctity . . . hand* – "heaven
has given his hand so much holy
power (*sanctity*) (that) . . ."

117 *They presently amend* – "they get
well at once".

No less in truth than life: my first false speaking 130
Was this upon myself.[102] What I am truly[103]
Is thine, and my poor country's, to command:[104]
Whither,[105] indeed, before thy here-approach,[106]
Old Siward,[107] with ten thousand warlike men,
Already at a point,[108] was setting forth. 135
Now we 'll together,[109] and the chance of goodness
Be like our warranted quarrel,[110] Why are you silent?

MACDUFF

Such welcome and unwelcome things at once,
'T is hard to reconcile.

Enter a Doctor[111]

MALCOLM

Well, more anon.
[*To the* Doctor] Comes the king forth, I pray you? 140

DOCTOR

Ay, sir; there are a crew[112] of wretched souls[113]
That stay his cure:[114] their malady convinces
The great assay of art;[115] but, at his touch,
Such sanctity hath heaven given his hand,[116]
They presently amend.[117]

MALCOLM

I thank you, doctor. 145

[*Exit* Doctor

MACDUFF

What 's the disease he means?

118 *A most miraculous work* – "it (the healing) is a most miraculous power".

119 *my here-remain* – "my stay"; compare *thy here-approach* in line 133 above.

120 *How he solicits . . . best knows* – "He himself knows best how he gains (*solicits*) (this power) from heaven."

121 *strangely-visited people* – "people suffering from strange diseases".

122 *mere* – "absolute".

123 *stamp* – "a coin", stamped with words and a picture of the king.

124 *'t is spoken* – "it is said (that)".

125 *the succeeding royalty* – "the kings and queens who follow him".

126 *The healing benediction* – "the holy gift of healing".

127 *With* – "Together with".

128 *sundry* – "various", i.e. other blessings, too.

129 *speak him full of grace* – "show him (to be) full of heavenly grace".

130 *My countryman*. Rosse must be wearing clothes which show him to be a Scot, for Malcolm calls him *My countryman*, yet does not recognise him.

131 *Good God . . . us strangers!* – "May God soon (*betimes*) remove the cause which makes us strangers", by allowing us to return in peace to our own country.

MALCOLM

      'T is called the evil:
A most miraculous work[118] in this good king,
Which often, since my here-remain[119] in England,
I have seen him do. How he solicits heaven,
Himself best knows;[120] but strangely-visited people,[121]   150
All swoln and ulcerous, pitiful to the eye,
The mere[122] despair of surgery, he cures;
Hanging a golden stamp[123] about their necks,
Put on with holy prayers: and 't is spoken,[124]
To the succeeding royalty[125] he leaves   155
The healing benediction.[126] With[127] this strange virtue
He hath a heavenly gift of prophecy;
And sundry[128] blessings hang about his throne
That speak him full of grace.[129]

Enter ROSSE

MACDUFF

      See, who comes here.

MALCOLM

My countryman;[130] but yet I know him not   160

MACDUFF

My ever-gentle cousin, welcome hither.

MALCOLM

I know him now. Good God betimes remove
The means that makes us strangers![131]

ROSSE

      Sir, amen.

132 *Stands Scotland where it did?* – "Is Scotland in the same condition as it was (when I left)?"

133 *where nothing . . . seen to smile* – "where no smile is ever seen except on those who (*But who*) know nothing (or what is happening)".

134 *not marked* – "not noticed", because there are so many noises of this sort.

135 *A modern ecstasy* – "an ordinary trouble of the mind", nothing exceptional or unusual.

136 *the dead man's . . . asked for who* – "when the bell is rung for a dead man, people hardly trouble to ask who (it is ringing for)".

137 *Dying or ere they sicken* – "dying before they fall ill". The flowers in men's caps die because they are pulled from their roots; men die too for reasons other than illness, and even more quickly now – i.e. they are murdered.

138 *relation* – "story".

139 *Too nice* probably means "very detailed". The account is full of unpleasant detail and too true to be comforting.

140 *the newest grief* – "the latest sorrow".

141 *That of an hour's . . . the speaker* – "(A grief) which is one hour old causes the man who tells of it to be hissed (by the hearers)", for they are certain to know it already; there are so many griefs, and they come so quickly that one which happened an hour ago is old.

142 *teems* – "brings forth".

MACDUFF

Stands Scotland where it did?[132]

ROSSE

          Alas, poor country!
Almost afraid to know itself. It cannot   165
Be called our mother, but our grave; where nothing,
But who knows nothing, is once seen to smile;[133]
Where sighs, and groans, and shrieks that rend the air
Are made, not marked;[134] where violent sorrow seems
A modern ecstasy:[135] the dead man's knell   170
Is there scarce asked for who;[136] and good men's lives
Expire before the flowers in their caps,
Dying or ere they sicken.[137]

MACDUFF

        O relation[138]
Too nice[139] and yet too true!

MALCOLM

        What's the newest grief?[140]

ROSSE

That of an hour's age doth hiss the speaker;[141]   175
Each minute teems[142] a new one.

MACDUFF

        How does my wife?

ROSSE

Why, well.

MACDUFF

        And all my children?

143 *a niggard of your speech* – "sparing in your words".

144 *heavily* – "with great difficulty".

145 *were out* – "had risen in rebellion (against Macbeth)".

146 *witnessed the rather* – "seen, rather (than just rumoured); seen in fact".

147 *For that* – "for the reason that".

148 *afoot* – "on foot, marching". The fact that Macbeth's army is on the march shows that there are forces rebelling against him.

149 *of* – "for".

150 *Your eye . . . create soldiers.* If Malcolm were to go to Scotland, he need only look at men to turn them into soldiers.

151 *To doff* – "to throw off".

152 *Be 't . . . coming thither* – "Let it, the fact that we are coming, be their comfort."

153 *An older and . . . gives out* – "Christendom makes known (*gives out*) no better or more experienced (*older*) soldier than he (Siward)."

154 *the like* – "similar (comfort)".

155 *would* – "should".

156 *Where hearing . . . latch them* – "Where no one is to hear, catch (*latch*) them."

186

ROSSE

Well, too.

MACDUFF

The tyrant has not battered at their peace?

ROSSE

No; they were well at peace when I did leave 'em.

MACDUFF

Be not a niggard of your speech:[143] how goes 't?   180

ROSSE

When I came hither to transport the tidings,
Which I have heavily[144] borne, there ran a rumour
Of many worthy fellows that were out;[145]
Which was, to my belief, witnessed the rather,[146]
For that[147] I saw the tyrant's power afoot.[148]   185
Now is the time of[149] help. Your eye in Scotland
Would create soldiers,[150] make our women fight
To doff[151] their dire distresses.

MALCOLM

                    Be 't their comfort,
We are coming thither.[152] Gracious England hath
Lent us good Siward, and ten thousand men;   190
An older and a better soldier none
That Christendom gives out.[153]

ROSSE

                    Would I could answer
This comfort with the like![154] But I have words
That would[155] be howled out in the desert air,
Where hearing should not latch them.[156]

157 *or is it a fee-grief . . . single breast?*;
lands held *in fee* are the property
of a single person; so a *fee-grief*
is a sorrow concerning one person
only – ". . . or is it a sorrow 'in
fee', concerning one heart only?"

158 *No mind . . . some woe* – "There
is no honest heart that will not
share some sorrow (with you)."

159 *possess them with the heaviest sound* –
"give them, put them in possession
of, the saddest sound".

160 *surprised* – "taken by surprise".

161 *to relate* (line 205) . . . *death of you* –
"to tell you the way (in which
they were killed) would be (*Were*)
to add your own death to the
killing (*quarry*) of these murdered
deer".

162 *ne'er pull . . . your brows* – "do not
pull your hat down over your
eyes". He is doing so perhaps to
cover up his tears.

163 *the grief . . . the o'er-fraught heart* –
"the sorrow that does not express
itself in words speaks in silence
(*Whispers*) to the over-weighted
heart". If he does not speak they
fear his heart will break.

MACDUFF

What concern they? 195

The general cause? or is it a fee-grief
Due to some single breast?[157]

ROSSE

No mind that 's honest
But in it shares some woe,[158] though the main part
Pertains to you alone.

MACDUFF

If it be mine,
Keep it not from me; quickly let me have it.   200

ROSSE

Let not your ears despise my tongue for ever,
Which shall possess them with the heaviest sound[159]
That ever yet they heard.

MACDUFF

Humph! I guess at it.

ROSSE

Your castle is surprised;[160] your wife and babes
Savagely slaughtered: to relate the manner   205
Were, on the quarry of these murdered deer,
To add the death of you.[161]

MALCOLM

Merciful heaven! —
What, man! ne'er pull your hat upon your brows:[162]
Give sorrow words; the grief that does not speak
Whispers the o'er-fraught heart,[163] and bids it break.   210

189

164 *And I must be from thence* – "And I had to be away from home (*from thence*) (when it happened)".

165 *I have said* – "I have said so (already)".

166 *Let 's make us ... deadly grief* – "Let us use our great (desire for) revenge as a medicine to cure this deadly sorrow." Here *medicines* and *cure* connect to form an image, and *us* simply means "for ourselves".

167 *He* probably refers to Malcolm; Macduff is mocking at him for saying "Be comforted" (line 213), for if Malcolm had children he would know that there could be no comfort then for Macduff. (But possibly Macduff is suggesting that if Macbeth had children he would murder them in revenge.)

168 *dam* – "mother".

169 *At one fell swoop.* This completes the image suggested by *hell–kite* (the devilish bird of prey, Macbeth) dropping on to the *pretty chickens* (Macduff's family) and killing them all in one cruel blow.

170 *Dispute it* – "Question it (in fighting)".

171 *I cannot but remember* – "I cannot help remembering (that)".

172 *such things*, the joys of family and home.

190

MACDUFF

My children too?

ROSSE

Wife, children, servants, all
That could be found.

MACDUFF

And I must be from thence![164]
My wife killed too?

ROSSE

I have said.[165]

MALCOLM

Be comforted:
Let 's make us medicines of our great revenge,
To cure this deadly grief.[166]   215

MACDUFF

He[167] has no children. – All my pretty ones?
Did you say all? – O hell-kite! – All?
What, all my pretty chickens, and their dam,[168]
At one fell swoop?[169]

MALCOLM

Dispute it[170] like a man.

MACDUFF

I shall do so;   220
But I must also feel it as a man:
I cannot but remember[171] such things[172] were,
That were most precious to me. – Did heaven look on,

173 *all struck for thee* – "all struck down, killed, because of you".

174 *Naught that I am* (line 225) . . . *on their souls* – "Slaughter fell on their souls not because of their own faults, but because of mine, and I am nothing (*Naught that I am*)".

175 *rest them* – "give them rest".

176 *Convert* – "be changed".

177 *play the woman* – "play the part of a woman" with his eyes, i.e. weep; to play the braggart with his tongue is to talk boastfully.

178 *all intermission* – "all pause (between this and revenge)".

179 *front to front* – "face to face".

180 *forgive him too*, as well as me, for letting him escape.

181 *This time goes manly; time* – "musical beat"; "this is a man's way of speaking", not the part of a woman such as Macduff spoke of in line 230.

182 *our power* – "our army".

183 *Our lack . . . our leave* – "we do not need anything except permission to go".

184 *Macbeth Is ripe for shaking*, as a fruit ready to be shaken off the tree.

185 *the powers . . . their instruments* – "the heavenly powers take on their arms (i.e. ourselves)".

186 *cheer* – "comfort".

187 *The night is . . . the day* – "It is indeed a long night which is never followed by day." In fact all nights are followed by days; the night of sorrow must at last end in the day of comfort.

And would not take their part? Sinful Macduff!
They were all struck for thee.[173] Naught that I am,   225
Not for their own demerits, but for mine
Fell slaughter on their souls:[174] heaven rest them[175] now!

MALCOLM

Be this the whetstone of your sword: let grief
Convert[176] to anger; blunt not the heart, enrage it.

MACDUFF

O! I could play the woman[177] with mine eyes,   230
And braggart with my tongue. – But, gentle heavens,
Cut short all intermission;[178] front to front[179]
Bring thou this fiend of Scotland and myself;
Within my sword's length set him; if he 'scape,
Heaven forgive him too![180]

MALCOLM

                    This time goes manly.[181]   235
Come, go we to the King: our power[182] is ready;
Our lack is nothing but our leave.[183] Macbeth
Is ripe for shaking,[184] and the powers above
Put on their instruments.[185] Receive what cheer[186] you may;
The night is long that never finds the day.[187]   240

                                                          [*Exeunt*

(v.i) Macbeth and his wife are now in the castle of Dunsinane. Lady Macbeth, greatly disturbed in her mind because of the crimes she and her husband have taken part in, walks in her sleep past a woman attendant, and a doctor who has been called in to watch her. As she walks she relives in words and actions some of the incidents she has experienced. When she has passed by, the doctor says that her mind, not her body, is sick, and that he is horrified at the truths he has learnt.

1 *Dunsinane.* The scene is laid in Macbeth's castle, where Lady Macbeth has, because of her troubled mind, been walking in her sleep.

2 *a Doctor of Physic* – "a Doctor of Medicine" (see illustration).

3 *watched* – "stayed awake".

4 *your report.* The gentlewoman has told the doctor of Lady Macbeth's sleep-walking.

5 *into the field* – "out with his army".

6 *closet* – "a cupboard in which valuable things can be kept safely".

7 *a most fast sleep* – "a very deep sleep".

8 *A great perturbation in nature* – "(It is) a great disturbance in life".

9 *do the effects of watching* – "do things which show (that she is) awake".

10 *slumbery* – "sleepy".

11 *other actual performances* – "other things she has actually done".

12 *That Sir, . . . after her* – "(I have heard her say) something, sir, which I shall not repeat".

13 *meet* – "proper (that)".

14 *having no witness . . . my speech* – "because I have no witness to confirm what I say (to be true)".

15 *taper* – "candle".

16 *Lo you!* – "Look!"

17 *her very guise* – "exactly her (usual) way".

18 *close* – "hidden".

Doctor of Physic[2]

194

ACT FIVE

Scene I. Dunsinane.[1] *A room in the castle.*
Enter a Doctor of Physic[2] *and a* Waiting-Gentlewoman.

DOCTOR

I have two nights watched[3] with you, but can perceive no truth
in your report.[4] When was it she last walked?

GENTLEWOMAN

Since his majesty went into the field,[5] I have seen her rise from
her bed, throw her night-gown upon her, unlock her closet,[6]
take forth paper, fold it, write upon 't, read it, afterwards seal it,   5
and again return to bed; yet all this while in a most fast sleep.[7]

DOCTOR

A great perturbation in nature,[8] to receive at once the benefit
of sleep, and do the effects of watching![9] In this slumbery[10]
agitation, besides her walking and other actual performances,[11]
what, at any time, have you heard her say?   10

GENTLEWOMAN

That, Sir, which I will not report after her.[12]

DOCTOR

You may to me; and 't is most meet[13] you should.

GENTLEWOMAN

Neither to you, nor any one, having no witness to confirm my
speech.[14]

Enter LADY MACBETH, *with a taper*[15]

Lo you![16] here she comes. This is her very guise,[17] and, upon   15
my life, fast asleep. Observe her: stand close.[18]

195

19 *How came she by* – "How did she get".

20 *their sense are shut; sense* must be taken as plural, "senses".

21 *Yet here 's a spot* – "There is still a spot (of blood) here".

22 *set down* – "write down".

23 *to satisfy . . . more strongly* – "to confirm more certainly what I remember (hearing)".

24 *One; two;* these must be two strokes of the bell, the signal for the murder of Duncan (II.i.62).

25 *Fie, my Lord, fie!* – She now imagines she is talking to Macbeth: "Shame, my Lord, shame!"

26 *afeard* – "frightened".

27 *none can . . . to account* – "no one can make us give an account of (how we use) our power".

DOCTOR

How came she by[19] that light?

GENTLEWOMAN

Why, it stood by her: she has light by her continually; 't is her command.

DOCTOR

You see, her eyes are open.   20

GENTLEWOMAN

Ay, but their sense are shut.[20]

DOCTOR

What is it she does now? Look, how she rubs her hands.

GENTLEWOMAN

It is an accustomed action with her, to seem thus washing her hands. I have known her continue in this a quarter of an hour.

LADY MACBETH

Yet here 's a spot.[21]   25

DOCTOR

Hark! she speaks. I will set down[22] what comes from her, to satisfy my remembrance the more strongly.[23]

LADY MACBETH

Out, damned spot! out, I say! — One; two;[24] why, then 't is time to do 't. — Hell is murky. — Fie, my Lord, fie![25] a soldier, and afeard?[26] — What need we fear who knows it, when none   30 can call our power to account?[27] — Yet who would have thought the old man to have had so much blood in him?

197

28 *mark* – "notice". Lady Macbeth in her disconnected talk reveals her memories of happenings that are secret to her and her husband.

29 *a wife.* This is Lady Macduff, who is dead.

30 *No more o' that.* Lady Macbeth is living again through the scene at which Banquo's ghost appeared (III.iv). She imagines she is talking to her husband – "(We want) no more of that (behaviour)."

31 *you mar all . . . starting* – "you will spoil everything (we have planned) with these shows of fear (starting)".

32 *Go to* – "Alas".

33 *you have known . . . should not.* The doctor is speaking as if to Lady Macbeth, or so the gentlewoman thinks; but what he says could also apply to her.

34 *spoke* for *spoken.*

35 *heaven knows* – "heaven may know (but I do not)".

36 *The heart is sorely charged* – "Her heart is full (of sorrow)."

37 *I would not . . . the whole body* – "I would not have a heart like that in my breast, not even for the worth (*dignity*) of the whole body."

38 *Well, well, well* – "Alas". But the gentlewoman misunderstands him, or at least plays upon his words; for in the next line she says, "(Let us) pray God that it *is* (well), sir", taking *well* to mean "in a good way".

39 *practice* – "skill".

40 *those* – "some people", who, although they walked in their sleep, had not a murder on their minds, and so died in peace.

198

DOCTOR

Do you mark[28] that?

LADY MACBETH

The Thane of Fife had a wife:[29] where is she now? – What,
will these hands ne'er be clean? – No more o' that,[30] my lord,   35
no more o' that: you mar all with this starting.[31]

DOCTOR

Go to,[32] go to: you have known what you should not.[33]

GENTLEWOMAN

She has spoke[34] what she should not, I am sure of that: heaven
knows[35] what she has known.

LADY MACBETH

Here 's the smell of the blood still: all the perfumes of Arabia   40
will not sweeten this little hand. Oh! oh! oh!

DOCTOR

What a sigh is there! The heart is sorely charged.[36]

GENTLEWOMAN

I would not have such a heart in my bosom for the dignity of
the whole body.[37]

DOCTOR

Well, well, well –[38]   45

GENTLEWOMAN

Pray God it be, sir.

DOCTOR

This disease is beyond my practice:[39] yet I have known those[40]

41 *Wash your hands.* It is the practical details that have stuck in Lady Macbeth's mind.

42 *on 's* – "of his".

43 *Even so?* – "Is it even as (bad as) this?"

44 *Foul whisp'rings are abroad* – "people are whispering terrible things to one another"; *abroad* – "current".

45 *Unnatural deeds . . . unnatural troubles.* In the first place *unnatural* means "wicked" – what is against nature, or not according to it, is bad. In the second place, "supernatural", a disease of the mind: "Wicked deeds breed supernatural troubles."

46 *discharge* – "throw off the weight of", hence "tell".

47 *More needs she the divine* – "She needs the priest (*divine*) (to confess her sins) more. . . ."

48 *the means of all annoyance* – "anything with which she can do herself harm".

49 *still keep eyes upon her* – "watch her always".

50 *mated* – "confused".

51 *amazed* – "disturbed".

which have walked in their sleep, who have died holily in their beds.

LADY MACBETH

Wash your hands,[41] put on your night-gown; look not so pale.
– I tell you yet again, Banquo's buried: he cannot come out   50
on 's[42] grave.

DOCTOR

Even so?[43]

LADY MACBETH

To bed, to bed: there 's knocking at the gate. Come, come,
come, come, give me your hand. What's done cannot be   55
undone. To bed, to bed, to bed.

[*Exit*

DOCTOR

Will she go now to bed?

GENTLEWOMAN

Directly.

DOCTOR

Foul whisp'rings are abroad.[44] Unnatural deeds
Do breed unnatural troubles:[45] infected minds   60
To their deaf pillows will discharge[46] their secrets.
More needs she the divine[47] than the physician. –
God, God forgive us all! Look after her;
Remove from her the means of all annoyance.[48]
And still keep eyes upon her.[49] – So, good-night: 65
My mind she has mated,[50] and amazed[51] my sight.
I think, but dare not speak.

201

(v.ii) Outside the castle of Dunsinane a force of loyal Scots is preparing to attack. They arrange to meet the English forces near the wood of Birnam.

1 The *drums and colours* are a sign that the army is moving out to fight.

2 *power* – "army".

3 *His uncle Siward.* Siward was not, in fact, Malcolm's uncle, but his grandfather. *Uncle*, however, was often used loosely in the English of Shakespeare's day to mean an older male relative.

4 *Revenges* – "Wishes for revenge".

5 *their dear causes* – "their reasons (for going to war) (*causes*), so dear to them, . . ."

6 *Would, to . . . mortified man* – ". . . would excite (even) the man whose feelings are quite dead (*mortified*) to grim and bloody war (*alarm*)".

7 *a file Of all the gentry* – "a list of all the important people (in this army)".

8 *unrough* – "smooth (in the face)", and therefore "tender, inexperienced".

9 *Protest their first of manhood* – "proclaim the first (signs of) their manhood".

GENTLEWOMAN

Good-night, good doctor.

[*Exeunt*

Scene II. The country near Dunsinane.

Enter, with drums and colours,[1] MENTETH, CATHNESS,
ANGUS, LENOX, *and Soldiers.*

MENTETH

The English power[2] is near, led on by Malcolm,
His uncle Siward,[3] and the good Macduff.
Revenges[4] burn in them; for their dear causes[5]
Would, to the bleeding and the grim alarm,
Excite the mortified man.[6]

ANGUS

        Near Birnam wood   5
Shall we well meet them: that way are they coming.

CATHNESS

Who knows if Donalbain be with his brother?

LENOX

For certain, Sir, he is not. I have a file
Of all the gentry:[7] there is Siward's son,
And many unrough[8] youths, that even now   10
Protest their first of manhood.[9]

MENTETH

       What does the tyrant?

CATHNESS

Great Dunsinane he strongly fortifies.

203

10 *that lesser hate him* – "who hate him less".

11 *He cannot buckle . . . belt of rule* – "He cannot buckle his disorderly (*distempered*) reasons (for fighting) within the belt of rule"; his ambitions are now so wild that they have become completely out of control, like a fat man with a stomach too big for his belt.

12 *Now minutely . . . his faith-breach* – "Now almost every minute (*minutely*) revolts upbraid him for his breach of faith."

13 *Those he commands . . . in love* – "The people whom Macbeth commands act only because they are commanded, and in no way (*Nothing*) because they love him."

14 *now does he . . . about him* – "he now feels that his right to the throne does not fit him as well as it did"; it is too big for him.

15 *His pestered senses* – "his troubled feelings".

16 *to recoil and start* – "if they jump and start".

17 *the medicine of the sickly weal* – "the man who will cure the illness of the state (*weal*)", Malcolm. This image, of a cure for an illness, is continued in the following lines with *pour*, *purge*, *drop* and even *sovereign* in line 30.

18 *in our country's purge* – "in the process of cleansing our country". It is as if they are a medicine poured into the country to cure it.

19 *dew the sovereign flower; sovereign* – both "royal" and "powerful as medicine" (thus continuing the image of healing; we speak in Modern English of a *sovereign remedy*): "sprinkle with dew, water, the sovereign flower". With the water they hope to make grow the true king of Scotland, Malcolm, and *drown the weeds*, Macbeth and his followers.

Some say he 's mad; others, that lesser hate him,[10]
Do call it valiant fury; but, for certain,
He cannot buckle his distempered cause   15
Within the belt of rule.[11]

ANGUS

                    Now does he feel
His secret murders sticking on his hands;
Now minutely revolts upbraid his faith-breach:[12]
Those he commands move only in command,
Nothing in love:[13] now does he feel his title   20
Hang loose about him,[14] like a giant's robe
Upon a dwarfish thief.

MENTETH

                    Who then shall blame
His pestered senses[15] to recoil and start,[16]
When all that is within him does condemn
Itself for being there?

CATHNESS

                    Well; march we on,   25
To give obedience where 't is truly owed:
Meet we the medicine of the sickly weal;[17]
And with him pour we, in our country's purge,[18]
Each drop of us.

LENOX

                    Or so much as it needs
To dew the sovereign flower[19] and drown the weeds.   30
Make we our march towards Birnam.

                                        [*Exeunt, marching*

(v.iii) Inside the castle Macbeth prepares for the siege. Messengers bring him news that the English force has arrived and is lined up against him. To Seyton he admits that his heart is heavy; he would have liked to hold his position with love and honour. The doctor tells him that he cannot help Lady Macbeth, since it is her mind which is diseased, not her body. But Macbeth bases his hopes on the witches' prophecies.

1 *Dunsinane*. The rest of the play consists of short scenes in which Macbeth prepares to fight and eventually leaves his castle to go out into the field; and it shows how Malcolm and the English forces move towards Dunsinane to meet him.

2 *let they fly all* – "let all of them (the soldiers who are leaving Macbeth and betraying his cause) fly".

3 *remove* – "moves".

4 *taint* – "go bad".

5 *All mortal consequence* – "everything that will happen to mortals in the future".

6 *pronounced me thus* – "said this of me".

7 *epicures* – "people living for the pleasures of the senses". The English appeared so to the Scots, who were themselves a hard, stern race.

8 *sway* – "rule".

9 *sag with doubt . . . with fear.* These clauses refer to *mind* and *heart* in the line before; the *mind* shall not droop (*sag*) with *doubt*, nor the *heart* know *fear*.

10 *thou cream-faced loon* – "you villain (*loon*) pale with fear". Macbeth curses the servant by asking that the devil (Satan) should damn him *black*, the colour of evil but also the opposite of white, the colour of fear shown on his face.

11 *Where gott'st . . . goose look?* – "Where did you get that goose look?", not only white but with "goose flesh" through fear.

12 *over-red thy fear* – "make your white face red (with blood)".

13 *Thou lily-livered boy.* The liver was thought to be the place in the human body from which came courage; Macbeth calls the servant's liver *lily* (-coloured), i.e. "white". What should have been red with courage was white with fear.

14 *patch* – "fool".

15 *counsellors to fear* – "advisers to fear (in others)"; his cheeks, the colour of linen, are so white that they put fear into the hearts of others.

16 *whey-face* – "face the colour of whey".

206

Scene III. Dunsinane,[1] *a room in the castle.*

Enter MACBETH, Doctor *and* Attendants.

MACBETH

Bring me no more reports; let them fly all:[2]
Till Birnam wood remove[3] to Dunsinane
I cannot taint[4] with fear. What 's the boy Malcolm?
Was he not born of woman? The spirits that know
All mortal consequence[5] have pronounced me thus:[6]   5
"Fear not, Macbeth; no man that 's born of woman
Shall e'er have power upon thee." – Then fly, false thanes,
And mingle with the English epicures:[7]
The mind I sway[8] by, and the heart I bear,
Shall never sag with doubt, nor shake with fear.[9]   10

Enter a Servant

The devil damn thee black, thou cream-faced loon![10]
Where gott'st thou that goose look?[11]

SERVANT

There is ten thousand –

MACBETH

Geese, villain?

SERVANT

Soldiers, sir.

MACBETH

Go, prick thy face, and over-red thy fear,[12]
Thou lily-livered boy.[13] What soldiers, patch?[14]   15
Death of thy soul! those linen cheeks of thine
Are counsellors to fear.[15] What soldiers, whey-face?[16]

207

17 *Seyton!* – Macbeth now calls a more trusted servant, Seyton, and to him he swears he will fight even though hope has gone.

18 *push* – "critical situation".

19 *Will cheer . . . me now* – "will (either) bring me happiness forever or unseat me (from the throne) at once". (Some play on words may be intended; *cheer* and *chair* had the same pronunciation in Shakespeare's English, and the idea of *chair* probably suggested *seat*, the throne.)

20 *my way of life . . . yellow leaf.* The image is of a leaf dropping, dry and yellow, from a tree in autumn; like this leaf, Macbeth's life has come to its autumn, and will soon fall: "The course of my life has fallen as a dry (*sere*) yellow leaf (in autumn)".

21 *accompany* – "go along with".

22 *As* – "such as".

23 *troops* – "great numbers".

24 *look* – "expect".

25 *in their stead* – "instead of them".

26 *mouth-honour* – "honour spoken but not felt; lip-service".

27 *breath*, i.e. words breathed but not meant.

28 *Which the poor heart would fain deny* – "which my poor heart would gladly reject (because they are not sincere)".

29 *and dare not* – "yet dare not", because all support, whether honourable or not, is now necessary.

208

SERVANT

The English force, so please you.

MACBETH

Take thy face hence. [*Exit* Servant] – Seyton![17] – I am sick at
  heart,
When I behold – Seyton, I say! – This push[18]   20
Will cheer me ever, or disseat me now.[19]
I have lived long enough: my way of life
Is fall'n into the sere, the yellow leaf;[20]
And that which should accompany[21] old age,
As[22] honour, love, obedience, troops[23] of friends,   25
I must not look[24] to have; but, in their stead,[25]
Curses, not loud but deep, mouth-honour,[26] breath,[27]
Which the poor heart would fain deny,[28] and dare not.[29]
Seyton! –

Enter SEYTON

SEYTON

What 's your gracious pleasure?

MACBETH

                What news more?   30

SEYTON

All is confirmed, my lord, which was reported.

MACBETH

I 'll fight, till from my bones my flesh be hacked.
Give me my armour.

SEYTON

              'T is not needed yet.

30 *skirr the country round* – "move quickly about the (surrounding) country".

31 *thick-coming fancies* – "fancies coming in great numbers".

32 *minister to a mind diseased* – "help (*minister to*) a diseased mind (as opposed to a diseased body)".

33 *Raze out* – "rub out (like words in a book)".

34 *oblivious* – "bringing forgetfulness".

35 *stuffed* – "filled completely full".

36 *physic* – "medicine; the art of healing".

37 *I'll none of it* – "I'll have none of it; it is useless to me."

38 *despatch* – "be quick".

39 *cast The water of my land* – "examine the urine (*water*) of my land", as if Scotland were a sick man, and the doctor could, by examination, find its disease and cure it.

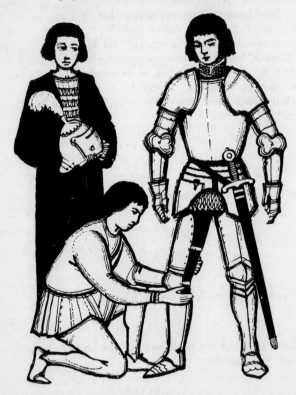

put mine armour on

210

MACBETH

I 'll put it on.
Send out more horses, skirr the country round;[30]   35
Hang those that talk of fear. Give me mine armour. –
[*To the* Doctor] How does your patient, doctor?

DOCTOR

Not so sick, my lord,
As she is troubled with thick-coming fancies,[31]
That keep her from her rest.

MACBETH

Cure her of that:
Canst thou not minister to a mind diseased,[32]   40
Pluck from the memory a rooted sorrow,
Raze out[33] the written troubles of the brain,
And with some sweet, oblivious[34] antidote
Cleanse the stuffed[35] bosom of that perilous stuff
Which weighs upon the heart?

DOCTOR

Therein the patient   45
Must minister to himself.

MACBETH

Throw physic[36] to the dogs; I 'll none of it.[37] –
[*To* SEYTON] Come, put mine armour on; give me my staff. –
Seyton, send out. – [*To the* Doctor] Doctor, the thanes fly from
    me. –
[*To* SEYTON] Come, Sir, despatch.[38] – [*To the* Doctor] If thou
    couldst, doctor, cast
The water of my land,[39] find her disease,   50
And purge it to a sound and pristine health,
I would applaud thee to the very echo,

211

40 *again* – "back". The applause would be so loud that it would echo back to the applauder.

41 *Pull 't off.* He is speaking to Seyton about a piece of his armour which has not fitted well.

42 *scour* continues the idea expressed in *purge*, line 52 above. The medicines he speaks of are used to clear poisons from the body. What can be used, he asks, to clear the poison of the English forces from the body of Scotland?

43 *Bring it after me* – "Follow me with it", *it* being, as in line 54, a piece of armour.

44 *bane* – "ruin".

(v.iv) Outside the castle the forces against Macbeth have now combined near Birnam wood; and, so that their numbers shall be concealed, Malcolm orders each soldier to cut down a branch from the trees and carry it in front of him.

1 *Enter, . . . marching.* It is apparent, from the people who now come on to the stage, that the English forces have come together as planned, and have joined up with the Scottish lords who are loyal to Malcolm. They are moving towards Dunsinane, the castle on the hill where Macbeth is ready to put up a last defence.

2 *chambers* – "bedrooms".

3 *We doubt it nothing* – "We do not doubt it at all".

That should applaud again.[40] – [*To* SEYTON] Pull 't off,[41] I say. –
[*To the* Doctor] What rhubarb, senna, or what purgative
   drug,   55
Would scour[42] these English hence? – Hear'st thou of them?

DOCTOR

Ay, my good lord: your royal preparation
Makes us hear something.

MACBETH

      [*To* SEYTON] Bring it after me.[43] –
I will not be afraid of death and bane[44]
Till Birnam forest come to Dunsinane.   60

                         [*Exit*

DOCTOR

[*Aside*] Were I from Dunsinane away and clear,
Profit again should hardly draw me here.

                       [*Exeunt*

Scene IV. Country near Dunsinane. A wood in view.

Enter, with drum and colours, MALCOLM, *old* SIWARD *and his* Son,
MACDUFF, MENTETH, CATHNESS, ANGUS,
LENOX, ROSSE, *and* Soldiers, *marching.*[1]

MALCOLM

Cousins, I hope the days are near at hand,
That chambers[2] will be safe.

MENTETH

      We doubt it nothing.[3]

SIWARD

What wood is this before us?

4 *thereby shall . . . our host* – "in this way we shall conceal (*shadow*) the size of our army".

5 *make discovery . . . report of us* – "cause the (men used by Macbeth on) observation (*discovery*) to make mistakes when they report on us".

6 *We learn . . . but* – "We hear nothing else but that."

7 *Keeps still* – "stays all the time".

8 *will endure . . . before 't* – "will bear (*endure*) our besieging (*setting down before*) it"; he will not give himself up.

9 *where there is advantage to be gone* – "(in every case) where there is an opportunity to get away".

10 *Both more and less . . . the revolt* – "both great and small people (i.e. those both more or less important) have revolted (and left his cause)".

11 *constrainèd things* – "wretched people who are forced (to serve him)".

12 *Whose hearts are absent too* – "and (even) their hearts are absent", for they have lost heart in the cause.

13 *Let our just . . . true event* – "Let our judgements (*censures*), if they are to be true (*just*) ones, wait until (*attend*) the actual event". It is useless to judge Macbeth's strength on hearsay alone.

14 *put we on* – "let us take on".

MENTETH
The wood of Birnam.

MALCOLM
Let every soldier hew him down a bough,
And bear 't before him: thereby shall we shadow   5
The numbers of our host,[4] and make discovery
Err in report of us.[5]

SOLDIERS
It shall be done.

SIWARD
We learn no other but[6] the confident tyrant
Keeps still[7] in Dunsinane, and will endure
Our setting down before 't.[8]

MALCOLM
            'T is his main hope;   10
For where there is advantage to be gone,[9]
Both more and less have given him the revolt,[10]
And none serve with him but constrainèd things,[11]
Whose hearts are absent too.[12]

MACDUFF
            Let our just censures
Attend the true event,[13] and put we on[14]   15
Industrious soldiership.

SIWARD
           The time approaches
That will, with due decision, make us know
What we shall say we have, and what we owe.
Thoughts speculative their unsure hopes relate,

15 *certain issue strokes must arbitrate* – "actual fighting (*strokes*) must judge (*arbitrate*), (giving) certainty to the result (*issue*)".

16 *advance the war* – "let the war advance".

(v.v) Macbeth, still confident in the strength of his castle, waits for the attack; but his fears return when he hears that his wife is dead. A messenger brings the news that Birnam wood appears to be moving. This persuades Macbeth that he can wait no longer. He commands his forces to prepare to leave the castle and fight.

1 *Hang out . . . outward walls.* Macbeth orders banners to be flown on the outside (*outward*) walls of the castle in order to show the enemy that those inside are prepared to fight.

2 *laugh a siege to scorn* – "laugh at a siege so much as to make it look beneath consideration" (see illustration).

3 *lie* – "settle".

4 *forced with . . . should be ours* – "strengthened (*forced*) with those (soldiers) who should be on our side".

5 *We might . . . them dareful* – "We might have met them with daring (*dareful*)".

6 *beard to beard* – "face to face".

7 *The time has . . . have cooled* – "There was a time when my senses would have turned cold".

8 *night-shriek* – "a shriek in the night".

9 *fell of hair* – "my hairy skin"; but what follows shows that here it simply means "hair", which "stood on end" when he heard a tale of horror.

10 *at a dismal treatise* – "on hearing a tale of horror".

11 *Direness* – "horror".

12 *start* – "frighten".

13 *Wherefore was* – "What was the reason for".

Our castle's strength
Will laugh a siege to scorn[2]

But certain issue strokes must arbitrate;[15]   20
Towards which advance the war.[16]

[*Exeunt, marching*

Scene V. Dunsinane. Within the castle.

Enter, with drum and colours, MACBETH, SEYTON, *and* Soldiers.

MACBETH

Hang out our banners on the outward walls;[1]
The cry is still, "They come!" Our castle's strength
Will laugh a siege to scorn;[2] here let them lie,[3]
Till famine and the ague eat them up.
Were they not forced with those that should be ours,[4]
We might have met them dareful,[5] beard to beard,[6]   5
And bear them backward home. [*A cry within, of women*] What
  is that noise?

SEYTON

It is the cry of women, my good lord.

[*Exit*

MACBETH

I have almost forgot the taste of fears.
The time has been, my senses would have cooled[7]   10
To hear a night-shriek;[8] and my fell of hair[9]
Would, at a dismal treatise,[10] rouse and stir,
As life were in 't. I have supped full with horrors:
Direness,[11] familiar to my slaughterous thoughts,
Cannot once start[12] me.

Re-enter SEYTON

Wherefore was[13] that cry?   15

217

14 *hereafter* – "after this".

15 *There would . . . such a word* – "There would have been a (better) time for such news (*a word*)."

16 *Tomorrow . . . petty pace* – "(Time) creeps along in such small movements (*petty pace*) – one tomorrow after another."

17 *the last syllable of recorded time* – "the last moment of time which will be recorded".

18 *all our yesterdays . . . The way* – "all the past days of our life have (only) given light to fools on the way". The idea of the light of life being a candle is continued in what follows.

19 *dusty death* – "death (which turns our bodies) to dust".

20 *brief* – "small, lasting for a short time". Life, like the light of a candle, quickly goes out.

21 *but* – "only".

22 *thy story* – "tell your news".

23 *As I did . . . upon the hill* – "As I stood on watch upon the hill". The *hill* must be inside the encircling wall of the castle, perhaps where the main tower stood.

SEYTON

The queen, my lord, is dead.

MACBETH

She should have died hereafter:[14]
There would have been a time for such a word.[15] –
Tomorrow, and tomorrow, and tomorrow,
Creeps in this petty pace[16] from day to day,   20
To the last syllable of recorded time;[17]
And all our yesterdays have lighted fools
The way[18] to dusty death.[19] Out, out, brief[20] candle!
Life 's but[21] a walking shadow, a poor player
That struts and frets his hour upon the stage,   25
And then is heard no more: it is a tale
Told by an idiot, full of sound and fury,
Signifying nothing.

Enter a Messenger

Thou com'st to use thy tongue; thy story[22] quickly.

MESSENGER

Gracious my lord,   30
I should report that which I say I saw,
But know not how to do 't.

MACBETH

Well, say, sir.

MESSENGER

As I did stand my watch upon the hill,[23]
I looked toward Birnam, and anon, methought,
The wood began to move.

24 *Let me endure your wrath* – "Let me bear (the consequences of) your anger".

25 *cling thee* – "dry you up".

26 *sooth* – "the truth, true".

27 *I care not . . . me as much* – "I do not care if you do the same (*as much*) for me", i.e. hang Macbeth on the nearest tree.

28 *I pull in resolution* – "I restrain my resolution (to continue with the fight)"; the image is of his resolution being pulled in like a horse.

29 *doubt* – "fear".

30 *the fiend* – "the enemy (of man); the devil". The drunken Porter said a good deal on the subject of equivocation (II.iii).

31 *Arm, arm, and out!* – "To your arms, and let us go out", out of the castle enclosure and into the field.

32 *does appear* – "shows itself in fact".

33 *There is nor . . . tarrying here* – "there can be neither running away nor staying (*tarrying*) here".

34 *aweary* – "tired".

35 *the sun* – "the light of the sun, life.

36 *th' estate o' th' world* – "the existence of the world".

37 *undone* – "destroyed".

38 *harness on our back* – "armour on our bodies", and therefore fighting.

(v.vi) Malcolm's forces throw down their branches and prepare to fight.

1 *show like those you are* – "show yourselves for what you are".

MACBETH

Liar and slave!   35

MESSENGER

Let me endure your wrath,[24] if 't be not so.
Within this three mile may you see it coming;
I say, a moving grove.

MACBETH

           If thou speak'st false,
Upon the next tree shalt thou hang alive,
Till famine cling thee:[25] if thy speech be sooth,[26]   40
I care not if thou dost for me as much.[27] –
I pull in resolution,[28] and begin
To doubt[29] th' equivocation of the fiend,[30]
That lies like truth: "Fear not, till Birnam wood
Do come to Dunsinane"; – and now a wood   45
Comes toward Dunsinane. – Arm, arm, and out![31]
If this which he avouches does appear,[32]
There is nor flying hence, nor tarrying here.[33]
I 'gin to be aweary[34] of the sun,[35]
And wish th' estate o' th' world[36] were now undone.[37] –   50
Ring the alarum bell! – Blow, wind! come, wrack!
At least we 'll die with harness on our back.[38]

                             [Exeunt

Scene VI. The same. A plain before the castle.

Enter, with drum and colours, MALCOLM, *old* SIWARD, MACDUFF,
etc., and their army, with boughs.

MALCOLM

Now, near enough: your leafy screens throw down,
And show like those you are.[1] – [*To old* SIWARD] You, worthy
  uncle,

2 *battle* – "army".
3 *take upon 's* – "make ourselves responsible for".
4 *According to our order* – "in accordance with the orders we have drawn up".
5 *Do we but find* – "If only we find".
6 *power* – "force, army".

(v.vii) In the field Macbeth meets Young Siward. They fight and Siward is killed. Macbeth recalls the prophecy of the witches, and goes to look for further victims. Macduff enters, looking for Macbeth. Malcolm and Old Siward bring the news that the castle has been surrendered.

1 *They have tied me to a stake.* Macbeth compares himself to a bear being "baited", i.e. ill-treated, maddened and eventually killed. Bear-baiting was a popular sport in Shakespeare's day; dogs were set on to a bear tied to a stake and baited it to death (see illustration).
2 *the course* – "a 'round' (in bear-baiting)".
3 *Such a one . . . or none* – "I must fear such a person (a man not born of woman) or nobody at all".
4 *Thou 'lt* is short for *Thou wilt* – "You will".

They have tied me to a stake[1]: I cannot fly,
But, bear-like, I must fight the course[2]

Shall, with my cousin, your right noble son,
Lead our first battle:[2] worthy Macduff and we
Shall take upon 's[3] what else remains to do,   5
According to our order.[4]

SIWARD

   Fare you well. –
Do we but find[5] the tyrant's power[6] tonight,
Let us be beaten, if we cannot fight.

MACDUFF

Make all our trumpets speak; give them all breath,
Those clamorous harbingers of blood and death.   10

     [Exeunt. Alarms continued

Scene VII. The same. Another part of the plain.

Enter MACBETH

MACBETH

They have tied me to a stake:[1] I cannot fly,
But, bear-like, I must fight the course.[2] – What 's he
That was not born of woman? Such a one
Am I to fear, or none.[3]

Enter young SIWARD

YOUNG SIWARD

What is thy name?

MACBETH

   Thou 'lt[4] be afraid to hear it.   5

5 *a hotter name . . . in hell; any is* –
"any that is". Hell is the place of
great heat, and the "hottest" name
there would be Satan's. Macbeth's
name is, in young Siward's ear, as
hateful as the devil's (line 8).

6 *swords I smile . . . a woman born* –
"I smile at swords and mock at
weapons which are brandished by
a man born of woman."

7 *be'st* – "be-est", the second person
singular, present subjunctive (after
if) of *to be*.

8 *still* – "for ever".

9 *Kernes* – Irish foot-soldiers who
fought for payment, not for a
cause.

YOUNG SIWARD

No; though thou call'st thyself a hotter name
Than any is in hell.[5]

MACBETH

My name 's Macbeth.

YOUNG SIWARD

The devil himself could not pronounce a title
More hateful to mine ear.

MACBETH

No, nor more fearful.

YOUNG SIWARD

Thou liest, abhorrèd tyrant: with my sword   10
I 'll prove the lie thou speak'st.

[*They fight, and young* SIWARD *is slain*

MACBETH

                    Thou wast born of woman: –
But swords I smile at, weapons laugh to scorn,
Brandished by man that 's of a woman born.[6]

[*Exit*

Alarms. Enter MACDUFF

MACDUFF

That way the noise is. – [*Calling to* MACBETH] Tyrant, show
    thy face:
If thou be'st[7] slain, and with no stroke of mine,   15
My wife and children's ghosts will haunt me still.[8]
I cannot strike at wretched Kernes,[9] whose arms

10 *either thou, Macbeth.* The sense of *I cannot strike* is carried on from the line before: "I cannot strike at wretched foot-soldiers ... but (I can) either (strike) at you, Macbeth, or ..."

11 *Or else ... again undeeded* – "or else I sheathe my sword again, unused (*undeeded*) and with its edge unbattered".

12 *There thou shouldst be* – "You must be *there*", at the place from which a great noise is coming.

13 *By this great ... Seems bruited* – "someone of the highest importance (*note*) seems to be proclaimed by this great noise (*bruited*)". The *clatter* is, perhaps, made by the soldiers beating their weapons together.

14 *the castle 's gently rendered* – "the castle has surrendered (*rendered*) quietly (to our forces)". Since Macbeth has left the castle, and is now in the field, the defences are weakened, and the surrender is *gentle*.

15 *The tyrant's people ... do fight* – "the tyrant's (Macbeth's) men are fighting on both sides", some for him and some against him.

16 *The day almost ... is to do* – "You have almost won the battle (*The day*), and there is little left to do."

17 *We have met ... beside us.* Either: (*a*) "We have met with soldiers from the enemy forces who are fighting at our side." Or (*b*) "... who (purposely) shoot on one side of us".

(v.viii) Macbeth meets Macduff. They fight and then pause, and there is time for Macduff to tell Macbeth how he was not, in a sense, "born of woman". They fight again and Macbeth is killed.

1 *play the Roman fool* – "play the part of a foolish Roman", e.g. Brutus or Antony, who killed themselves with their own swords.

2 *On mine own sword*, i.e. by falling on to it.

3 *Whiles I see ... upon them* – "Whilst I see (other) people alive (*lives*), wounds are more fitting on *them* (than on *me*, who thought of dying by my own hand)."

Are hired to bear their staves: either thou, Macbeth,[10]
Or else my sword, with an unbattered edge,
I sheathe again undeeded.[11] There thou shouldst be;[12]   20
By this great clatter, one of greatest note
Seems bruited.[13] [*Aside*] Let me find him, Fortune!
And more I beg not.

[*Exit. Alarm*

Enter MALCOLM *and old* SIWARD

SIWARD

This way, my lord; – the castle 's gently rendered:[14]
The tyrant's people on both sides do fight;[15]   25
The noble thanes do bravely in the war.
The day almost itself professes yours,
And little is to do.[16]

MALCOLM

We have met with foes
That strike beside us.[17]

SIWARD

Enter, Sir, the castle.

[*Exeunt. Alarm*

Scene VIII. Another part of the field.

Enter MACBETH

MACBETH

Why should I play the Roman fool,[1] and die
On mine own sword?[2] Whiles I see lives, the gashes
Do better upon them.[3]

227

4 *Turn* – "Turn round!" Macduff, hunting down Macbeth to take vengeance on him, has come up behind him on the stage, and surprised him.

5 *charged With* – "weighed down with responsibility for".

6 *blood of thine*, i.e. the blood of Macduff's family.

7 *thou bloodier . . . thee out!* – "you villain bloodier than words (*terms*) can proclaim you (*give thee out*)!"

8 *Thou losest labour* – "You waste your effort", because no man born of woman can harm Macbeth.

9 *As easy may'st . . . sword impress* – "you may as easily (*easy*) strike (*impress*) the air, which cannot be cut (*intrenchant*), with your sharp sword, as . . ."

10 *Let fall thy blade . . . crests* – "let the blade of your sword fall upon crests which can be injured" (see illustration).

11 *must not* – "cannot".

12 *Despair thy charm* – "Despair of, put no trust in, your charm".

13 *the angel whom . . . hast served* – "the angel whom you have always served", viz a spirit of wickedness, not a good angel.

14 *it hath cowed . . . of man* – "it has disheartened the better part of my manhood", not the bodily, but the spiritual part, where a man's courage lies.

on vulnerable crests 10

Enter MACDUFF

MACDUFF

Turn,[4] hell-hound, turn!

MACBETH

Of all men else I have avoided thee:
But get thee back, my soul is too much charged
With[5] blood of thine[6] already.

MACDUFF

            I have no words;
My voice is in my sword: thou bloodier villain
Than terms can give thee out![7]

                       [*They fight*

MACBETH

           Thou losest labour:[8]
As easy may'st thou the intrenchant air
With thy keen sword impress,[9] as make me bleed:
Let fall thy blade on vulnerable crests:[10]
I bear a charmèd life, which must not[11] yield
To one of woman born.

MACDUFF

         Despair thy charm;[12]
And let the angel whom thou still hast served[13]
Tell thee, Macduff was from his mother's womb
Untimely ripped.

MACBETH

Accursèd be that tongue that tells me so,
For it hath cowed my better part of man:[14]
And be these juggling fiends no more believed,

15 *palter with us in a double sense* –
"equivocate with us", by keeping
the word of a promise but not its
spirit.

16 *yield thee* – "give yourself up".

17 *the show and gaze o' th' time* – "the
object of show and gaze of all the
world (*th' time*)".

18 *rarer monsters* – "stranger animals".

19 *Painted upon a pole*. Pictures of
strange animals and other things
(e.g. the *painted devil* in II.ii.54)
were painted on cloth or board and
fixed to a pole for people to look
at.

20 *underwrit* – "(with the title) written
beneath".

21 *To kiss ... Malcolm's feet*, i.e. to
honour him as king of Scotland.

22 *And thou opposed ... woman born* –
"and (although) you, being of no
woman born, (are) opposed (to
me)".

23 *before my body ... warlike shield* –
"I thrust (*throw*) my shield, ready
for battle, in front of my body."

24 *lay on, Macduff* – "come and fight,
Macduff".

25 *damned be him that* – "let him be
damned who ..."

26 *Hold* – "Stop".

(v.ix) Inside the castle Malcolm and
the loyal forces take stock of the
day's losses. These have not been
great, but Young Siward has died
a soldier's death. Macduff is missed,
but he soon enters, carrying Macbeth's head; he is able to greet Malcolm as king of Scotland. Malcolm
makes his thanes and kinsmen earls,
promises to take revenge on Macbeth's allies, and invites them all to
see him crowned.

1 *Retreat* – "Trumpet-call at the end
of a battle".

2 *I would ... safe arrived* – "I wish
the friends we miss had arrived
safely."

3 *go off* – "be killed".

4 *these* – the thanes and soldiers around
him.

That palter with us in a double sense,[15]   20
That keep the word of promise to our ear,
And break it to our hope. – I 'll not fight with thee.

MACDUFF

Then yield thee,[16] coward,
And live to be the show and gaze o' th' time:[17]
We 'll have thee, as our rarer monsters[18] are,   25
Painted upon a pole,[19] and underwrit,[20]
"Here may you see the tyrant".

MACBETH

                    I will not yield,
To kiss the ground before young Malcolm's feet,[21]
And to be baited with the rabble's curse.
Though Birnam wood be come to Dunsinane,   30
And thou opposed, being of no woman born,[22]
Yet I will try the last: before my body
I throw my warlike shield:[23] lay on, Macduff;[24]
And damned be him that[25] first cries, "Hold,[26] enough!"

> [*Exeunt, fighting. Alarms. Re-enter fighting,*
> *and* MACBETH *is slain.*

Scene IX. Within the castle.

Retreat.[1] Flourish. Enter, with drum and colours,
MALCOLM, *old* SIWARD, ROSSE, Thanes *and* Soldiers.

MALCOLM

I would the friends we miss were safe arrived.[2]

SIWARD

Some must go off;[3] and yet, by these[4] I see,
So great a day as this is cheaply bought.

231

5 *He only lived* (line 6) . . . *man he died* – "He lived only until he became a man. And his courage (*prowess*) had no sooner confirmed this (that he had reached manhood) in the place where he fought and from which he did not fall back (*unshrinking*), than, like a man, he died."

6 *hath* – "would have".
7 *before* – "in front". His wounds were in front of his body, which showed that he died fighting and not running away.
8 *wish them to a fairer death* – "wish a better death for them".

MALCOLM

Macduff is missing, and your noble son.

ROSSE

Your son, my lord, has paid a soldier's debt: 5
He only lived but till he was a man;
The which no sooner had his prowess confirmed,
In the unshrinking station where he fought,
But like a man he died.[5]

SIWARD

Then he is dead?

ROSSE

Ay, and brought off the field. Your cause of sorrow
Must not be measured by his worth, for then   10
It hath[6] no end.

SIWARD

Had he his hurts before?[7]

ROSSE

Ay, on the front.

SIWARD

Why, then, God's soldier be he!
Had I as many sons as I have hairs,
I would not wish them to a fairer death:[8]   15
And so, his knell is knolled.

MALCOLM

He 's worth more sorrow,
And that I 'll spend for him.

233

9 *parted* for *departed*.

10 *paid his score* – "paid his bill", the *soldier's debt* in line 5 above.

11 *the time* – "the world, the people".

12 *compassed with thy kingdom's pearl* – "surrounded (*compassed*) by your chosen men, your thanes"; *thy kingdom's pearl* refers to what is precious, chosen in the kingdom, the chosen men of Scotland.

13 *That speak . . . in their minds* – "who repeat my greeting (*Hail, King!* in line 20) in their minds".

14 *we reckon . . . even with you* – "I calculate (*reckon with*) what each of you has done to show his love (for me) (*your several loves*), and make myself equal (*even*) with you." Malcolm is indebted to the thanes for help, and will pay them back quickly (without *a large expense of time*) with honours.

15 *What 's more to do* – "Whatever else there is to be done". And Malcolm goes on to give some examples of the things which are to be carried out; by this he shows he intends to rule wisely and well.

16 *Which would be . . . the time* – "which must be put into effect in accordance with the changed circumstances (*newly with the time*, Macbeth being king no longer)".

17 *That fled . . . watchful tyranny* – "who fled from the traps of a tyrant always watching them".

18 *Producing forth* – "bringing out (for punishment)".

19 *ministers* – "helpers, advisers".

20 *by self and violent hands* – "by her own fierce hands".

21 *Took off her life* – "killed herself".

22 *what needful else* – "whatever else is necessary".

23 *the grace of Grace* – "the grace of God".

24 *in measure, time and place* – "in a reasonable way, at (the proper) time and place".

SIWARD

He 's worth no more;
They say he parted[9] well, and paid his score:[10]
And so, God be with him! – Here comes newer comfort.

Enter MACDUFF *with* MACBETH'S *head.*

MACDUFF

Hail, King! for so thou art. Behold, where stands   20
Th' usurper's cursèd head: the time[11] is free.
I see thee compassed with thy kingdom's pearl,[12]
That speak my salutation in their minds;[13]
Whose voices I desire aloud with mine, –
Hail, King of Scotland!

ALL

. Hail, King of Scotland!   25
                                                      [*Flourish*

MALCOLM

We shall not spend a large expense of time
Before we reckon with your several loves,
And make us even with you.[14] My thanes and kinsmen,
Henceforth be earls, the first that ever Scotland
In such an honour named. What 's more to do,[15]   30
Which would be planted newly with the time,[16] –
As calling home our exiled friends abroad,
That fled the snares of watchful tyranny;[17]
Producing forth[18] the cruel ministers[19]
Of this dead butcher, and his fiend-like queen,   35
Who, as 't is thought, by self and violent hands[20]
Took off her life;[21] – this, and what needful else[22]
That calls upon us, by the grace of Grace,[23]
We will perform in measure, time and place.[24]
So thanks to all at once, and to each one,   40
Whom we invite to see us crowned at Scone.

                                                      [*Flourish. Exeunt*

GLOSSARY

This glossary explains all those words in the play which are used in Modern English as they were in Shakespeare's day, but are not among the 3,000 most-used words in the language.

The notes opposite the text explain words which are *not* used in Modern English. In these notes it has been necessary to use a very few words which are also outside the 3,000 word list; these are included in the glossary.

Explanations in the glossary are given entirely within the chosen list of words, except in the few cases where a word is followed by *q.v.*; this shows that the word used will itself be found explained elsewhere in the glossary.

Only the meaning of the word *as used in the text or notes* is normally given.

v. = verb; n. = noun; q.v. = "see this (word)".

A

abhor, hate.
abide, stay.
abound, be abundant.
abuse, use badly.
accent, (n.) a greater force given to a part of a word in speaking; (v.) to give this force. (E.g. in the word *Macbeth*, the accent falls on the second syllable, Macbéth; we accent the second syllable.)
access, a way of entering.
accompany, go with.
accursed, lying under a curse, devilish.
adage, a saying.
adder, a small poisonous snake.
adhere, support firmly.
adieu, good-bye.
afflict, cause pain.
agent, force, power.

agitate, makes anxious.
ague, fever from cold.
aid, help.
alarum (now usually spelt *alarm*), warning of danger.
alas! is a cry of sorrow.
alembic, an instrument used in chemistry for *distilling* (q.v.).
allegiance, loyalty.
amen, "May it be so". The word is used at the end of a prayer.
angel, a messenger from God.
anoint, put oil on a person (e.g. a king when he is crowned, as a sign that he is made sacred).
anticipate, look forward to something before it comes or happens.
antidote, a medicine which acts against a poison.
appal, fill with fear.
apparition, a ghost.
appease, make quiet, calm.

arbitrate, decide (in a disagreement).

assailable, that can be attacked.

assassination, murder arising from disloyalty.

assault, a violent attack.

assure, say for certain.

audience, people watching a play in the theatre.

audit, check accounts (to see that they are right).

auger, a tool for boring small holes.

augment, increase.

avarice, greed (for money and other possessions).

avouch, declare to be true.

B

baboon, a kind of large monkey.

badge, a mark worn to tell something about the wearer, e.g. that he is a member of a club.

bait, worry so as to make angry.

balm, a comforting medicine or influence.

bark, ship.

barren, unproductive, (of women) unable to have children.

bat, a small animal like a mouse which flies at night.

batter, hit violently and often.

battlement, a wall on the roof of a castle with openings through which soldiers could shoot.

beer is a drink.

beetle, an insect with hard shining wing-covers.

beguile, deceive.

behold, see.

besiege, attack a place (e.g. a castle) from all sides in order to capture it.

beware, be careful of.

bid, (simple past tense sometimes *bade*), ask, command.

bird-lime, a sticky substance used for catching birds.

blanch, to become white, pale.

blanket, a soft woollen covering used on beds; and, from this, any covering, e.g. *a blanket of snow*.

blaspheme, speak about God or sacred things in a bad and disrespectful way.

bleed, lose blood.

blister, raise small swellings of the skin, filled with a liquid like water.

bonfire, a large fire made out-of-doors.

bosom, the human breast.

botch, spoil because of bad work.

bounty, generosity.

brag, boast.

braggart, boaster.

brandish, wave about.

breach, an opening or space made in a wall.

breeches, trousers.

brew, any drink prepared by boiling, mixing, etc.

broil, quarrel.

broth, water in which meat has been boiled.

buckle, to fix a fastener joining two loose ends.

buffet, (a blow, and from this) a misfortune.

buttress, a support built against a wall.

C

calendar, a list of days, weeks and months of the year.

cancel, do away with, wipe out.

cannon, a large gun.

capital, punishable by death.

carouse, drink much and be merry.

cask, a barrel for holding liquids.

catalogue, a list of names.

cauldron, a large pot in which things may be boiled or cooked.

censure, blame.

chalice, a ceremonial cup.

challenge (for), call or invite to dispute in some way (because of).

chamber, a bedroom.

chamberlain, an official in the household of a king.

champion, support another person in a cause, e.g. by fighting or speaking.

chastise, punish severely.

cherub, an imaginary child, beautiful and innocent, with wings on its shoulders.

chestnut, the fruit of the chestnut tree, a sweet nut.

chide, scold.

choke, to stop the breath of a person by pressing the windpipe from outside or blocking it inside.

chorus, words said, or a song sung, by a number of people at the same time.

Christendom, Christian countries.

cistern, tank.

clamour, loud, confused noise.

clatter, the confused sound of hard objects knocking together.

clause, a part of a sentence, with a subject and predicate of its own, but doing the work of a noun, adjective or adverb.

cleave, stick fast (this use is old-fashioned except in the form *cleave to* – "be faithful to").

cling, hold fast.

clog, fill up (e.g. with dirt), so as to prevent easy movement.

cloister, a covered walk by a church.

clutch, take tight hold of (something) with the hand.

compass, an instrument with a needle which always points north and south.

compliment, an expression of praise or admiration.

compunction, a feeling of regret or hesitation concerning something one is going to do.

conference, a meeting at which people exchange ideas and opinions.

confirm, show the truth of something which has been said.

conspire, make a secret plan to do something unlawful.

constancy, firmness, the quality of being unchangeable.

contend, struggle.

contradict, say that what is said or written is not true.

contrast, compare one thing with another in such a way that the differences are seen.

contrive, plan or make cleverly.

corporeal, of the body.

corrupt, in a bad state.

counsel, advise.

counterfeit, something copied and false.

county, a large division of land made for the purposes of local government.

covet, desire greatly (especially a thing which belongs to someone else).

crave, ask earnestly for.

crazed, mad.

creation, the world; the universe.

crest, the top of a helmet (q.v.).

crib, keep in a small space.

cricket, a small brown insect that makes a noise by rubbing its wings together.

croak, make a low, rough sound.

crow, a large black bird which cries Caw! Caw!

cur, a worthless dog.

cut-throat, murderer.

D

dagger, a pointed knife used as a weapon.

damn, condemn to ruin or destruction.

daring, bravery.

dash, knock to pieces.

daunt, frighten; and so *dauntless*, very brave.

dedicate, show or say that something is to be used for a particular purpose.

defect, fault.

defile, spoil the purity or cleanness of (something).

delinquent, one who does wrong or neglects his duty.

desolate, lonely, wretched.

despatch, kill.

detract, make less, specially in value or honour.

digest (of food), to change after eating for use in and by the body.

diminutive, very small.

dire, terrible.

disaster, a terrible misfortune.

disburse, pay.

disdain, look down on, scorn.

dismal, sad.

dismay, a feeling of hopelessness.

distil, change a liquid into a gas and back again to a liquid, so as to purify it (see note 65 to I.vii.).

distracted, confused.

divulge, make known (especially a secret).

downy, soft.

drab, bad woman.

drama, the branch of literature concerned with plays for the theatre.

dramatic, like a drama; sudden and exciting.

dramatis personae (Latin), "the people of the drama", a list of characters in the play.

draw, pull out (e.g. a sword).

dread, fear.

dregs, what is found at the bottom of a liquid (e.g. wine), when it has been left standing for some time.

drench, make thoroughly wet.

drowse, be half asleep.

dun, dull greyish-brown.

dung, the waste material dropped by animals.

dwarf, a person much smaller than the normal size.

dwindle, grow smaller.

E

earl is the title of an English nobleman.

eclipse, a partial darkening of the sun or moon.

economy, using what one has carefully so that nothing is wasted.

ecstasy, a state of very strong feeling, especially of joy.

e.g., for example.

elf, a small fairy, imagined as living in caves or woods.

embrace, accept.

enchant, use magic on.

enforce, compel.

enterprise, a plan, especially one that requires courage.

entrails, the inside parts of an animal.

entreat, ask or beg earnestly.

exaggerate, say that something is larger, better, more important, etc., than it really is.

exasperate, anger greatly, make a person completely lose his patience.

execute, put to death according to the law.

exeunt (Latin), they go off (the stage).

exile, send (a person) away from his country as a punishment.

exit (Latin), he, she goes off (the stage).

expire, come to an end.

exploit, bold or adventurous act.

F

falcon, a meat-eating bird once used to kill other birds and small animals.

famine, extreme scarcity of food.

farrow, all the young of a pig which are born at one time.

feat, an act showing great bravery or strength.

fee, give a payment for services.

fell, terrible (used in Modern English only in the phrase *one fell swoop*, which is directly borrowed from *Macbeth*).

fie! for shame!

fiend, a devil.

fillet, a thick piece of meat without bone.

filth, dirt.

flourish, showy music played (e.g. on trumpets) to make known the arrival or departure of an important person.

flout, mock at.

fog, a thick mist.

foot, a division of a line of poetry, each division having one heavy *syllable* (q.v.).

forge, make dishonestly and with difficulty.

forth, out into general view.

fortify, make strong.

fortitude, calm courage in times of trouble.

frank, showing one's thoughts or feelings freely.

fret, worry.

frieze, an ornamental band of stone along a wall.

fulsome, excessive and insincere.

fume, a strong gas.

function, the natural activity of something (e.g. the body).

furbish, polish.

G

gall, the bitter liquid made in the body by the liver (q.v.).

gash, a deep, long wound.

gentlewoman, a lady, particularly one serving a queen or other woman of high rank.

gibbet, a wooden frame on which bodies of criminals used to be shown after hanging.

glare, stare fiercely.

glimmer, give out a weak, unsteady light.

gloss, brightness.

glossary, a list of difficult words, with notes and explanations.

gore, blood that has become thick.

Gospels, the first four books of the New Testament in the Bible, which describe the life and teachings of Jesus.

graft, put a shoot from one plant or tree into another in order to make a new growth.

grapple, struggle.

greyhound, a long-legged dog, able to run fast.

grim, severe.

groom, an attendant.

grove, a group of trees.

gruel, a liquid food usually made of oatmeal boiled in water or milk.

guardian, a person who takes care of someone's life and property as a duty.

gum, the flesh round the teeth of men and animals.

H

hack, cut roughly.

hag, an ugly old woman.

hail, greet; *Hail!* is used as a greeting.

harbinger, a person or thing that makes known what is coming.

hatch, produce secretly.

hautboy, (the sound of the) oboe, a musical wood-wind instrument.

hawk, a strong swift bird of prey.

heath, an area of waste open land.

helmet, a piece of armour for covering the head.

hemlock, a plant from which a poisonous drink may be made.

henbane, a poisonous plant.

herald, make known the coming of (someone).

hew, cut.

hideous, very ugly.

hilt, the handle of a dagger.

hiss, show dislike by making a sound like that of s.

hoarse, rough (in voice).

homage, the formal offering of loyalty and service to a lord by a man beneath him.

horrid, terrible.

horror, a strong feeling of fear and dislike.

hound, a dog used for hunting.

house-martin, a bird like a swallow which nests on the walls of houses.

hover, remain in or near one place in the air.

hurlyburly, noisy disorder.

I

idiot, a fool.

i.e., that is.

illusion, something that deceives the mind; a false idea.

impede, hinder.

imperial, of an empire (Scotland is thought of as an empire in *Macbeth*).

implore, beg earnestly.

impostor, a person who pretends to be what he is not.

incense, a substance producing a sweet smell when burned; it is burned as part of a ceremony in some churches.

indissoluble, that cannot be broken up; lasting.

infect, poison or fill with disease.

infirm, weak.

ingredient, one of the parts of a mixture, especially in the preparation of food.

inhabitant, a person who lives in a certain place.

inhibit, restrain.

insane, mad.

integrity, the state of a person being honest, good and sincere.

intemperance, the state of lacking self-control.

interdiction, forbidding, especially by keeping a person out of or away from something.

interim, a period of time, especially that between two events.

interpret, explain the meaning of.

invest, give a person the outward signs of a title or honour.

irony, saying what one wants to say by using words which normally mean the direct opposite of what one really intends to suggest; e.g.:

DUNCAN
Dismayed not this
Our captains, Macbeth and Banquo?

CAPTAIN
Yes;
As sparrows eagles, or the hare the lion.

Dramatic irony arises when the audience is aware of some fact that a character is unaware of.

issue, children.

J

jovial, merry.

judicious, wise.

juggle, play tricks.

K

kinsman, a male relative.

kite, a bird of prey, with a forked tail and long wings.

knell, a bell rung solemnly at the time of death.

knoll, ring a bell.

L

lace, a fine ornamental material made in various net-like designs.

lament, show or feel great sorrow.

laudable, deserving praise.

lechery, an act of evil desire.

lees, the thick parts of wine that settle at the bottom of a container.

leisure, time free from work or duty.

levy, a number of men forced to do military service.

liege, a lord entitled to receive service and *homage* (q.v.).

lime; see *bird-lime*.

liver, a large organ in the body which helps the changing of food into blood.

lizard, a kind of small animal with a long body and tail, and four legs.

lowly, humble.

lust, evil desire.

M

magpie, a black and white bird with a long pointed tail; it has a very noisy call.

malady, illness.

malevolence, desire to do evil to other people.

malice, desire to harm other people.

manhood, the state of being a man; the qualities that belong to a man.

mankind, the human race.

mar, spoil.

marrow, the soft, fatty substance that fills the central part of bones.

marshal, guide, lead.

marvel, show wonder or surprise.

masterpiece, something done with very great skill.

meek, mild and gentle.

melody, a tune (in music).

messenger, one who carries a message.

metaphor, the use of words in such a way that they mean something quite different from what is normal; e.g., a lion is an animal, but it is possible to say, "The man was a lion in the fight", meaning that he fought like a lion.

mew, to make the sound made by a cat.

miracle, a wonderful happening, especially one which seems to take place contrary to the laws of nature.

mischance, a piece of bad luck.

monastery, building in which a group of men live a religious life away from the world.

mongrel, a dog of mixed breed.

monster, any very large animal; and so, a person who is remarkable for some very bad quality.

monstrous, horrible.

mould, a model according to which something is shaped.

mummy, the body of a human being preserved from decay.

munch, eat with a great deal of movement in the jaws.

murky, dark and cheerless.

N

navel, a mark or small hollow near the middle of the body.

negative, that which denies, says "No".

nerve, courage; nerves are connections between parts of the body and the brain.

newt, a small animal like a lizard (q.v.), which spends most of its time in the water.

nimble, quick and active (in body or mind).

nipple, that part of the breast through which a baby gets its mother's milk.

nourish, give food to.

O

obedience, obeying.

obscure, dark, not clear.

o'erleap; see *overleap*.

oppression, cruel or unjust rule.

oracle, the answer given to a question about what will happen in the future; the person who answers such a question.

orphan, a child who has lost one or both parents by death.

outrun, run faster than.

overleap, jump too far.
overtake, catch up with.

P

pall, a heavy black cloth.
palpable, that can be felt or touched.
palter, be insincere in what one says.
parley, meeting to discuss terms.
parricide, murder of a parent or near relative.
peal, a loud ringing of bells.
peerless, without equal.
peg, a wooden screw for holding and tightening the strings of a musical instrument.
pendent, hanging.
penthouse, a shelter with a sloping roof attached to a building.
perfume, a sweet-smelling liquid made from flowers.
peril, danger.
pernicious, destructive.
persevere, keep on doing (even though the act may be difficult).
pertain, belong, relate to.
perturb, disturb.
petty, small and unimportant.
piglet, a baby pig.
pilot, a person who guides a ship.
pine, waste away through sorrow or illness.
pious, religious.
pit-fall, a trap for animals to fall into
plight, a bad condition.
pluck, pull out.
poodle, a small pet dog.
positive, that which is not negative (q.v.), which says "Yes".
posterity, all the descendants of a person.
potent, powerful.
prate, talk foolishly.
prattle, talk like a child, in a simple, innocent way.
predecessor, one who has held a position before another.
predict, foretell.

predominant, above others (e.g. in strength, numbers).
prefix, a syllable placed in front of a word to add to its meaning.
primrose, a plant, common in England, with pale yellow flowers.
pristine, original.
probation, a trial or testing of suitability.
procreant, related to the having of children.
prologue, an introduction (to something greater).
prophecy, a foretelling.
prophesy, foretell.
prose, ordinary written language, not poetry.
provoke, excite, awaken.
prowess, courage.
purge, clean by clearing away what is bad.
pyramid, a structure square at the bottom, with four triangular sides.

Q

quench, put out; bring to an end by satisfying.
quotation, words used which have already been written or spoken by someone else.

R

rabble, disorderly crowd of people.
rancid, not fresh (e.g. of fat).
rapt, giving all one's attention to something.
ratify, make certain.
raven, a large black bird.
ravish, violate (a woman or girl).
receptacle, vessel or space which holds or contains something.
recompense, reward.
reconcile, bring (facts, for example) into agreement.
redress, put right.
reek, smell badly.

relish, flavour.

remorse, a feeling of guilt.

repent, feel very sorry (for some wrongdoing).

requite, give in return.

resolute, determined.

resound, fill a place with sound.

retainer, one who serves a person of high rank.

revolt, rise in rebellion.

rhinoceros, a large, heavy, thick-skinned animal.

rhubarb, a garden plant with thick stems which can be cooked.

riddle, a puzzling question.

rook, a large black bird, very much like a crow.

round, one of a series of contests, as in boxing (see note 2 to v.vii.).

rouse, awaken, disturb into action.

ruby, a red precious stone.

rugged, rough.

rumour, a statement or story talked of as news, without any proof that it is true.

S

sacrilege, the crime of treating a sacred person or thing with disrespect.

sag, sink down.

salutation, greeting.

salute, a friendly greeting.

sauce, a liquid served with food to improve its taste.

saucy, rude.

scarf, a long piece of cloth worn round the neck.

sceptre, the staff carried by a king as a sign of his power.

scorpion, a small creature found in hot countries; it has eight legs, and a tail with a poisonous sting.

scour, make very clean or bright.

scruple, an uneasiness in the mind, felt until something is done or while something has not been done.

seam, the line made when two pieces of cloth are joined together.

sear, dry up.

senna, the dry leaves of a plant (cassia), used as medicine.

sentinel, one who watches and gives warning in case of danger.

sere, dried (especially of plants, flowers and leaves).

sergeant, an officer in the army.

serpent, a snake; and so, an untrustworthy person.

service, a set of dishes, etc., used in serving a meal.

shark, a large fish, often very fierce.

sheathe, put (e.g. a sword) into its case or covering.

shed, make flow (e.g. blood).

shoal, a great number.

shrink, move or draw back.

siege, the surrounding of a fortified place by an army to force it to give up. (For *fortified*, see under *fortify* in this glossary.)

sieve, an instrument used for separating things of different sizes.

skull, the bony framework of the head.

slain; see *slay*

slaughter, killing, especially of animals.

slay, kill (past participle *slain*).

sleek, make smooth.

smear, mark with something sticky or dirty.

smother, cover, particularly cover a person so as to cause difficulty in breathing.

snore, loud breathing coming from a person who is asleep.

sole, single.

solicit, beg for.

sovereign, possessing the highest power.

sow, a female pig.

spaniel, a dog with large, drooping ears; it is renowned for its faithfulness.

244

sparrow, a common, small, brown-ish-grey bird.

speculate, consider carefully.

sponge, the light framework of a dead sea animal which is soft and so takes up water.

sprite, a spirit, fairy.

spur, urge on (as a rider urges on a horse by pricking its sides with *spurs*).

spurn, refuse as being unworthy.

stab, pierce or wound with a weapon such as a dagger.

stall, a shed for horses or cattle.

start, make a sudden movement (as from pain or fear).

statute, fixed law.

stave, a strong stick, e.g. for a spear.

stealthy, cautious, done with great secrecy.

steep, make very wet, bathe.

stool, a seat without a back.

strangle, kill a person by pressing hard on the throat.

streak, a long, irregular line of colour.

stride, walk with long, swinging steps.

strut, walk in a proud, self-important way.

subtle, difficult to describe or explain.

sundry, various.

sup, eat supper.

supernatural, not capable of being explained by the ordinary laws of nature; beyond what is natural.

surfeit, cause to take too much of something, especially food or drink.

surgeon, a doctor who carries out operations.

surgery, the work of treating illnesses and injuries by operation.

surmise, supposition.

surrender, stop fighting against an enemy.

survey, look at carefully.

swift, quick.

swine, pig, pigs.

swinish, beastly.

swoln, an old form of *swollen*, grown bigger.

syllable, a word or part of a word spoken with a single effort of the voice.

T

tangle, a confused mass of thread, hair, etc.

tarry, wait, stay.

tedious, long and uninteresting.

temperance, self-control in speech and behaviour.

tempest, a violent storm with much wind.

thane, a member of a class between nobles and ordinary freemen in early English and Scottish history.

theme, a subject on which one speaks, writes or thinks.

thrall, a slave.

thrice, three times.

thrift, careful control in the spending of money.

throb, beat strongly or rapidly (e.g. the heart).

tiger, a large, fierce animal of the cat family; it has yellow fur striped with black.

toad, a small animal like a frog.

topple, fall through unsteadiness.

torch, a flaming light, made e.g. by a burning piece of wood.

torture, deliberately cause great pain to.

tragedy, a play in which the chief characters are driven by circumstances or by their own nature to great suffering.

traitor, one who helps the enemies of his country.

treacherous, disloyal.

treason, disloyalty in important matters to one's king and country.

treble, threefold.

trench, cut a ditch.

trifle, a thing of little importance or value.

tug, pull with great force.

tyranny, cruel or unjust use of power.

tyrant, a cruel or unjust ruler.

U

ulcer, an open wound from which poisonous matter comes.

unruly, disorderly; difficult to control.

unsanctified, unholy.

untimely, not happening at the normal time.

upbraid, scold.

urine, the liquid collected in the body and then discharged.

usurp, take possession of (something, e.g. power) wrongfully.

V

valiant, brave.

valour, bravery.

vanquish, overcome, defeat.

vantage (for *advantage*): used in phrases such as *point of vantage*, a strong position from which to fight.

vapour, gas which heat produces from a liquid.

vault (1), n. an arched roof.

vault (2), v. jump in a single movement.

venom, poisonous liquid given out by some snakes and insects.

verity, truth.

vile, morally bad.

villain, one who has done, or may do, great evil.

villainy, great evil.

vouch, support the certainty of.

vulnerable, that can be wounded.

vulture, a large bird of prey; and so an evil, greedy person who takes advantage of those weaker than himself.

W

wade, walk through water.

wanton, wild, uncontrolled.

warder, a prison guard.

wayward, wilful.

whetstone, a stone used for sharpening edged tools, e.g. knives.

whey, the liquid part left after cheese has been made from milk.

whine, make a low, long-drawn, complaining cry.

whore, a mistress.

womb, the organ of a woman's body in which children are held before birth.

wrack, ruin.

wren, a small short-winged bird.

wrench, pull suddenly and violently.

Y

yawn, open the mouth wide, as when sleepy.

yell, give a loud, sharp cry, as with pain.

yew, an evergreen tree, often planted in churchyards.

HINTS TO EXAMINATION CANDIDATES

(Prepared by H. M. Hulme, M.A., Ph.D.)

This section is intended to offer some help to candidates who are studying *Macbeth* for such examinations as School Certificate or G.C.E., Ordinary Level, and who are working alone. Actual questions from London papers are used as examples to show the kinds of question that may be found on most papers for examinations at this stage.

You will see first that you must know the story of the play in some detail. Secondly, you must give yourself practice in reading the questions carefully and answering exactly what is asked; *do not expect to find on any paper a question that you have already answered*. Thirdly, you must train yourself to write quickly enough to finish the work in the time allowed (30 minutes for each of these sample questions). Do not waste time, for example, in copying out the question.

See to it that you know beforehand which kinds of question you *must* do and which you *may* do. For some examinations (e.g. London) you must do one "context" question and you may also do an essay question on the set play; for others you may have some choice between "context" and essay questions.

"CONTEXT" QUESTION

Sample question from London University, G.C.E., Ordinary Level, Summer 1959.

1. Choose ONE of the following passages and answer the questions below it.

EITHER—

(i)

Lady Macbeth: Give him tending,
              He brings great news.   (*Exit Attendant.*)
                                   The raven himself is hoarse
              That croaks the fatal entrance of Duncan

Under my battlements. Come you spirits
That tend on mortal thoughts, unsex me here,
And fill me from the crown to the toe top-full
Of direst cruelty; make thick my blood,
Stop up th' access and passage to remorse,
That no compunctious visitings of nature   10
Shake my fell purpose . . .

(a) Who is to be given "tending" (l. 1) and why? What is the great news he brings?

(b) What was Lady Macbeth's "fell purpose" (l. 11)? What had prompted this intention?

(c) Give, in your own words, the meaning of "no compunctious visitings of nature shake my fell purpose" (ll. 10–11).

(d) What is meant by "spirits that tend on mortal thoughts" (ll. 5–6) and "th' access and passage to remorse" (l. 9)?

(e) Say briefly how Duncan's later arrival at Macbeth's castle contrasts with this speech of Lady Macbeth.

OR—

(ii)

Macbeth: To be thus is nothing,
But to be safely thus—our fears in Banquo
Stick deep, and in his royalty of nature
Reigns that which would be feared. 'Tis much he dares,
And to that dauntless temper of his mind,   5
He hath a wisdom, that doth guide his valour
To act in safety. There is none but he
Whose being I do fear; and under him
My Genius is rebuked, as it is said
Mark Antony's was by Caesar. He chid the sisters,   10
When first they put the name of King upon me . . .

(a) Where did Macbeth speak these words and what action was he contemplating?

(b) How did Banquo chide the sisters (l. 10) and when did he and Macbeth meet them?

248

(c) Explain "his royalty of nature" (l. 3) and "a wisdom that doth guide his valour to act in safety" (ll. 6–7).

(d) What is meant by:
> "under him
> My Genius is rebuked as, it is said,
> Mark Antony's was by Caesar" (ll. 8–10)?

(e) What did the sisters tell Banquo and what does Macbeth say later in this speech to show that this had deeply disturbed him?

NOTES ON POSSIBLE ANSWERS

Notes on (i)

(a) A messenger; he is exhausted with riding quickly ahead. Duncan is coming to Macbeth's castle that night.

(b) To persuade Macbeth to murder Duncan.
His letter, telling of the witches' prophecy that he should become king and describing how the prophecy that he should be Thane of Cawdor had already come true.

(c) "No feelings of human kindness shall prick my conscience and turn me from my savage plan."

(d) "Witches and supernatural creatures who watch over and help those who are planning murder."
"All the ways through which repentance and pity might come into my heart."

(e) Duncan described the castle as a pleasant place; martins are nesting there, which is a sign of summer. Lady Macbeth has spoken of the ravens, a sign of death and danger.

Attempt one passage only.
Note that a good deal of accurate information is necessary here. Write as simply and shortly as possible. Number the sections carefully. See that you have not left out any of the "bits", e.g. (a) Why? (b) What had prompted this intention? (d) "th' access and passage to remorse".

(c) A question which begins with "Give, in your own words" requires a neatly arranged answer which will make clear, by re-wording, the meaning of *compunctious*, *visitings*, *nature*, *shake*, *fell*, *purpose*. Do not use in your answer any of these given words or words formed from them e.g. *compunction*, *natural*. Try out your attempt in pencil first; your final version should be written out clearly without any crossings out.

(d) For a question which begins with "What is meant by ..." you may allow yourself a few extra words of explanation, e.g. for *spirits*, "witches and supernatural creatures".

(e) Try to give two or three points for this section.

Notes on (ii)

(a) In his royal palace; giving orders for the murder of Banquo.

(b) By saying that he was not afraid and asking for the truth. Just after their victory over the rebels.

(c) "Kingly nobleness of character." He is to be the father of many kings.
"Good sense which shows him how to act bravely without putting himself into unnecessary danger."

(d) "Banquo's guardian spirit is more powerful than mine, just as, in Roman history, it is said that Julius Caesar had a stronger personality than his friend, Mark Antony."

(e) They told Banquo that he should be the ancestor of kings, although not himself a king. Macbeth regrets that he has no son and that he has murdered Duncan only so that Banquo's children shall be kings.

Answer only what is asked. In (b) say when, but not *where*; in (e) what did the sisters tell Banquo (not Macbeth). For (c) and (d) re-word carefully; both are difficult; for these two sections only try out your attempt in pencil first.

Essay Questions

2. "In the play we see Macbeth first and last as a fighting soldier." (a) Contrast the impressions you have of Macbeth at the opening and at the end of the play, and (b) say why, in your opinion, Shakespeare lets Macbeth end his life as a brave soldier.

3. "The play ranges over many human emotions." Show by close reference to *one* appropriate scene or episode for *each* how in this play Shakespeare conveys or portrays *two* of the following: (a) fear, (b) pity, (c) horror, (d) ruthlessness.

Each of these questions requires *detailed knowledge* of the play.

Jot down *brief notes* before you begin to write. Remember that you will certainly not have time to write out the whole essay in rough and then copy it out later. Plan carefully: the way in which the question is arranged will tell you how to plan your answer.

Any quotations given should be short; do not waste time on long quotations of ten or twenty lines; it is more important to show that you yourself can write simply and clearly. When quoting poetry, quote in lines and begin the quotation about one inch from the left-hand margin. The quotations given should fit grammatically into your own sentences.

NOTES ON POSSIBLE ANSWERS

Question 2

Plan: Note that *Contrast* means "Show the differences between". Give two-thirds of your time to (a) which asks for your knowledge of the play, and one-third to (b) which asks for "your opinion". Since (a) is rather a large section, divide this into two paragraphs. The first paragraph could be on Macbeth as a soldier (points 1 to 4), and the second on Macbeth as a soldier influenced by the witches.

Material: at the opening: up to the meeting with the witches; *at the end:* from the moving of Birnam wood.

Arrangement:

(*a*) Make your *contrast* rough jottings in two columns. You will need three of these points for a moderately good essay, five for really good work.

at the opening	*at the end*
1. With Banquo.	Without friends.
2. Fighting for king and country against rebels and invaders from Norway.	Himself the king, but Scottish and English forces against him.
3. Fearless.	Sick at heart.
4. Praised by many. Fights more bravely as new forces come against him.	Hated by all. Decides to stay inside his castle. Many soldiers have deserted him and his army is too small to fight in battle.
5. Startled by the witches' prophecy; ready to believe it because he is already thinking of the throne.	Hearing of the approach of Birnam wood begins to fear that the witches have tricked him. Goes out to fight.

(*b*) Keep the rest of the end of the play for section (*b*), your third paragraph. Find two or three sensible reasons; four are suggested below with blanks left for you to fill in.

1. Macbeth does not kill himself, as X is said to have done, because he is a soldier.

2. The last prophecy is fulfilled when he fights against X.

3. Justice is done when Macduff takes vengeance for ——.

4. Scotland will have, once more, a strong king, since X wins the throne by battle.

Begin the first paragraph at once without an introduction; you can earn marks only for information given, e.g.

At the beginning of the play Macbeth, with Banquo, is fighting for his king and country against Scottish rebels and

252

the Norwegian invaders. At the end, by contrast, he has no friends, and, although he himself is king, almost all Scotland is against him and the English have invaded Scotland to join against him.

(Keep to one tense, either present or past, throughout your essay. Write briefly. You have a lot to say.)

Question 3

Plan: The audience or the readers feel those emotions which Shakespeare *conveys*; the characters on the stage feel the emotions which he *portrays*. (Since the question says "conveys or portrays" and does not emphasise "or" by printing it *or*, you are free to take either one or both of these, as you wish.) Write two long paragraphs for each of the emotions you choose. Use a *different* scene or episode ("part of the story") for each.

Material: This writer will choose the *pity* which the audience feels in seeing the sleep-walking scene; the *horror* which Macbeth, and the audience, feel in the banqueting scene, and will write first on *horror* because the banqueting scene comes earlier in the play.

Arrangement:

(c) *Horror.* Do not simply tell the story of this scene. Choose certain points, e.g.:

the description of the murdered Banquo; neither the murderer nor Macbeth has any pity for him; Macbeth's pretence that he wanted Banquo to come; the timing of the ghost's entrance; Macbeth's description of the ghost; the strain on Lady Macbeth.

(b) *Pity*

Lady Macbeth dare not sleep without light; although she washes her hands, she cannot wash away the thought of the murders; she remembers much. Even the doctor and the gentlewoman pity her.

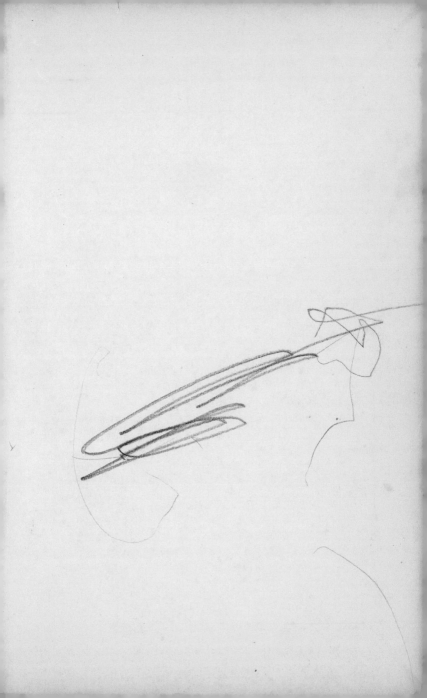

Job interview Questions, Tips & advie